5Q Daily

The 2022 Collection

SANAT PAI RAIKAR

DEDICATION

To A and B, for showing me the path.

To N and S, for walking the path with me.

To QoT, who knew all the answers.

CONTENTS

ACKNOWLEDGMENTS

This book compiles the questions from the 5Q Daily website hosted by Sanat Pai Raikar and includes all questions from 2022. 5Q Daily has received a wonderful response in its first year. For this, there are many people to thank.

Firstly, my wife and daughter, who bear with my constantly interrupting them with my daily set of questions. Their encouragement and support mean the world to me.

I would also like to thank our extended families for their support and constant encouragement while working on this book.

I want to thank my fellow quizzers and quizzing groups for their feedback, motivation, and validation of the question samples I kept throwing their way. My quiz groups are a key portion of my life and I owe thanks to all of you. Special thanks to the Quizzers of Tredence who attempted every question I threw at them.

And lastly, I want to thank you, the reader and my fellow quizzer, for picking up this book and reading it.

i

SET 1: WEEKS 1-10

1. What was discovered in 1901 at the ancient site of Susa, in present day Iran, by Egyptologist Gustave Jequier? It had 244 items in the Cuneiform script, arranged in 44 columns and 28 paragraphs.

2. What was the then English Premier League chairman Richard Scudamore talking about when he said, "If this was a once in every 5,000-year event, then we've effectively got another 5,000 years of hope ahead of us?"

3. Which fictional family resides in Skypad apartments in Orbit City, where people commute in aerocars with transparent bubble tops?

4. What connects the islands of Jan Mayen, Iceland, Azores, Saint Peter and Paul Rocks, Ascension Island, Saint Helena, Tristan da Cunha, Gough Island and Bouvet Island?

5. What real-life 1962 event is referenced in the main battle scene in the superhero film 'X-Men: First Class'?

6. Which strategically important city, that has been battled over more than a hundred times throughout history, and whose name means 'White city' in the local language, was the location of the first Non-Aligned Movement conference in 1961?

7. What water body, whose name roughly translates as 'Sea of Islands', once had 1000+ islands that dotted its waters? Part of its former coverage area is now a desert region.

8. Which former capital of a European country continues to hold an unofficial status as a second capital, and served as the seat of government for 9 years after the capital was moved to its present location?

9. The plot of which graphic novel written by Alan Moore begins on 05 November 1997 in London?

10. Chris Evans is very well known for portraying Captain America in the Marvel Cinematic Universe films. But which other Marvel Comics character has he portrayed on film?

11. Which town is depicted as medium-sized, and as having beaches, lakes, rivers, deserts, farmland, woods, mountains, a transit system and four distinct seasons? Most of the residents we know attend the 11th grade.

12. Which actor, famous for his role in another film franchise, is known among DC Comics

fans for voicing the supervillain Joker in animated films and video games for over two decades?

13. The male Aldabra giant tortoise Adwaita, who died at the age of 255 in the Alipore Zoological Gardens of Kolkata in 2006, originally lived on whose estate in the Northern Kolkata suburbs?

14. The town of Tharangambadi was originally established in 1620 as the first trading post of which European country in India?

15. The islands of Bombay famously came to the British as part of the dowry of the Portuguese princess Catherine of Braganza when she married Charles II of England. England then leased the islands to the English East India Company for what sum in 1668?

16. The Commonwealth Games are played among athletes from the British Commonwealth. What Games are played by countries having a history with Portugal?

17. The United States is the clear leader in the all-time medals tally at the Summer Olympics. As of 2020, which country led the all-time tally at the Winter Olympics?

18. Who has been described by the University Central Hospital in Helsinki, Finland as lacking the 17 to 22 percent body fat required for a woman to menstruate? Her bathroom scale from 1965 was permanently set at 110 pounds, which is 35 pounds underweight for a woman of her height.

19. Which science fiction and detective fiction writer, a recipient of an honorary doctorate from Oxford University, was also a publisher, illustrator, and calligrapher, but was most well-known for his work in films?

20. The first Indian sportsman to be nominated to the Rajya Sabha (upper house) of Parliament, which professional wrestler was best known for his on-screen portrayal of Hanuman?

21. The year 1642 saw the death of a prominent engineer and scientist in January. December of the same year saw the birth of another mathematician and scientist. The former is known for his discovery of several celestial bodies, while the latter is known for formulating laws explaining the behavior of such bodies. Name both.

22. Which well-known film and theatre artist, also a Rhodes scholar and Jnanpith awardee, wrote the Kannada plays Yayati and Nagamandala?

23. The 1978 film *I Wanna Hold Your Hand* by director Robert Zemeckis was about the fans of which music group?

24. What two-word term connects the epigraph of the EM Forster novel Howards End and a British television quiz show hosted by Victoria Coren Mitchell?

25. What unit of measurement represents the standard length of a furrow on a square field of ten acres in medieval times?

26. The 1980 Wimbledon Mixed Doubles title was won by Tracy Austin and John Austin. What

first did they achieve?

27. Which mammal was 'found' by the French missionary and naturalist Pere Armand David in China in 1869?

28. Which decisive battle, fought in 1415, was a key event in the Hundred Years War, and is notable for use of the English longbow in large numbers?

29. In the first century BC, the second Roman Triumvirate was Lepidus, Mark Antony and which other statesman?

30. Which of Lord Krishna's sobriquets is earned because his mother used to tie him around his belly to prevent him from doing mischief?

31. Which English word, meaning bizarre, comes from the Italian word for cave, in an allusion to certain caves in Rome, where paintings of this style were found?

32. Which US city holds the world's oldest annual race, instituted in 1897?

33. Frelimo was the party leading the independence movement and subsequent governance in which African nation?

34. The ring of small icy bodies orbiting the sun beyond the outermost planets of the solar system is named after which American astronomer who proposed their existence?

35. The dreaded Tonton Macoute was the secret police of which Caribbean country in the 1960s?

36. In which town was the German Republic established under the Constitution of 1919,

before being finally overthrown in 1933?

37. The name of which US public-opinion statistician has now become a generic term for sample surveys of public opinion?

38. Which metallic element was named by miners using the German word for Goblin, because it was poisonous and degraded other elements such as nickel?

39. The rules for which sport were laid down by the Marquis of Queensbury in 1868?

40. Which animal, known for its vertical leaps, is the sporting emblem of South Africa?

41. By what name is Abhas Kumar Ganguly known in Indian cinema?

42. How do we better know the condition called *circadian rhythm stress*?

43. What is the Esperanto word for amazing, also the name of a popular soft drink brand?

44. What soft drink brand was formulated by CL Grigg in 1929, and originally called 'Bib-Label Lithiated Lemon-Lime Soda'?

45. What soft drink, originally marketed as a mixer for whiskey, derived its name from a slang word for moonshine (homemade liquor)?

46. Originally an Iranian subsidiary of Pepsi, it became a standalone corporation following the 1979 Iranian Revolution. Which drink, named after one of the stops on the Islamic pilgrimage of the Haj, am I talking about?

47. What discovery did the German chemist Friedrich Kekule make while having a dream on a bus in 1865?

48. What sporting slogan was coined by the French Dominican preacher Henri Didon in 1891?

49. Who is the Roman goddess of flowers and of the season of spring?

50. What business term derives from the Latin for *broken bench*?

51. Who was Head of State of India, from its independence on 15 August 1947, to 26 January 1950, when its Constitution came into effect, and it became a full-fledged republic?

52. Which jurist, economist and social reformer is known as the 'Father of the Constitution of India'?

53. 26 January was chosen as the date for Republic Day because it was on this day in 1929 that the Indian National Congress proclaimed what?

54. Which arterial road in New Delhi was built in honor of George V's visit to Delhi in 1911, and was subsequently renamed post-independence to its current name?

55. Which Bharat Ratna awardee's autobiography is called *Wings of Fire*?

56. What three letter word connects a snake famously used to commit suicide, and a web framework?

57. Which rock band is known, among other things, for providing music to the films *Flash Gordon* and *Highlander*?

58. Connect a song by Boney M, the X-Man Colossus, and a famous Russian mystic. Single word answer.

59. Which country's national anthem is known in English as "The hymn of the isthmus"?

60. What term, meaning 'intoxicated', is used to describe a phenomenon wherein an oily substance is secreted from pores near the eyes of the Indian elephant?

61. Muhammad-bin-Tughlaq, the then Sultan of Delhi, tried to shift the imperial capital from Delhi to Devagiri. What did he rename it as?

62. If Elvis Presley lived in the *Graceland* estate, who lived in the *Neverland* estate?

63. The Mughal Empire is mainly known for the rule of six rulers from Babur to Aurangzeb, before it started to decline. Who is the only one amongst them to be buried in Delhi?

64. Which Indian scientist demonstrated radio wave transmission at the Presidency College in Kolkata (then Calcutta) in 1894?

65. What nickname was given to James J Braddock, a dockworker who was World Heavyweight Boxing champion from 1935 to 1937?

66. US diplomat Ralph Bunche became the first black person to win the Nobel Peace Prize in 1950, for his peace efforts in which disputed region?

67. Which 11th century Indian king is known for crossing the Bay of Bengal and conquering states in parts of present-day Indonesia and Malaysia?

68. In which country was Prime Minister Mahendra Chaudhury ousted in a coup by

George Speight in the year 2000?

69. In the Federer-Nadal-Djokovic dominated period from 2005 to the present day (Jan-2022), only 2 men have won 3 Grand Slam singles titles. One is Stan Wawrinka. Who is the other?

70. What is the Sanskrit term for 'the abode of peace', also the seat of a famous university in India?

71. Which patron saint of France has her traditional feast day celebrated on May 30, the day she was executed?

72. Marie Curie was the first woman to win a Nobel prize in a science category in 1903. In 1911, who became the second woman to win a science category Nobel prize?

73. The Zubrowka Bison Grass vodka brand, known for vodka bottles containing a bison grass blade, is from which country?

74. Which member of Emperor Akbar's court was born as Mahesh Das, and was known as 'Kavipriya' until a new name was bestowed upon him?

75. Which African country was formerly known as French Sudan until its independence in 1960?

76. What connects the international airports in New Delhi, Varanasi, Hyderabad, and Lucknow?

77. Which English cricket captain was born in Madras (now called Chennai) in 1968?

78. Who was labeled by Time magazine as 'king of cybercommerce', when he was named Person

of the Year in 1999?

79. Ashleigh Barty won the Australian Open Women's Singles title last weekend. Who was the last Australian woman to win the Australian Open Singles title, doing so in 1978?

80. How do we better know the Indian actor Muhammad Kutty Panaparambil Ismail?

81. The Indian states of Gujarat and Maharashtra were formed in 1960 from which former state?

82. Which gin-based cocktail was invented by a bartender working at the Long Bar in the Raffles Hotel?

83. The Spanish exclaves of Ceuta, Melilla and Penon de Velez de la Gomera border which country, which claims the territories they enclose?

84. Which literary classic was originally titled *Elinor and Marianne*?

85. Under what name does Taiwan (also called *Republic of China*) compete in the Summer and Winter Olympic Games?

86. Which author, the first novelist to feature on British currency, is known for books which feature poor social or working conditions?

87. Which is the only astrological sign not personified by a living thing?

88. If the Radcliffe Line separates India and Pakistan, which Line separates Pakistan and Afghanistan?

89. The 1993 film *Cool Runnings* is loosely based on the story of which country's bobsleigh team debut at the 1988 Winter Olympics?

90. Which country leads the all-time medals tally in the Winter Olympics?

91. The 1994 Winter Olympic Games in Lillehammer, Norway marked the first time the Winter and Summer Olympics were held in separate years (two years apart). Which famous exhibit was stolen from the Oslo National Museum during the opening ceremony, due to poor security on account of focus on the Olympic festivities?

92. Which location in New York state, a two-time Winter Olympics host, shares its name with a horror film series?

93. Which novel, published a 100 years ago in February 1922, covers events occurring in the protagonist's life on 16 June 1904?

94. William Morgan invented the sport of *Mintonette* after being influenced by James Naismith and basketball. Morgan wanted a less vigorous sport more suited to older members, but still requiring athletic skill. How do we know *Mintonette* today?

95. In the 2006 film *Casino Royale*, James Bond is on an assignment to bankrupt the terrorist financer Le Chiffre by beating him in a game of poker. Which game is played in the original Ian Fleming novel *Casino Royale*?

96. Which city is the 2010 video game *Assassin's Creed: Brotherhood* set in?

97. Which 1853 memoir by Solomon Northup became a best-seller 160 years later, thanks to an Oscar winning film adaptation?

98. Which city is the subject of the William Dalrymple book *City of Djinns*?
99. Queen Elizabeth II's coronation took place on 2 June 1953. India's Prime Minister at the time was Jawaharlal Nehru. Who was the US President?
100. Who was born as Farrokh Bulsara in 1946 to Parsi-Indian parents, and did most of his schooling in boarding schools in India?
101. The 1958 film *The Hidden Fortress* by Akira Kurosawa tells the story of two peasants who escort a princess across enemy lines in return for gold. Which hugely popular science fiction film from the 1970s did it heavily influence?
102. In Jules Verne's *Journey to the Center of the Earth*, the protagonists begin their journey from the Snaefellsjökull volcano in Iceland. At which Mediterranean volcano does their journey end?
103. In the 2021 film 83 based on India's win at the 1983 Cricket World Cup, Kapil Dev is portrayed by Ranveer Singh. Who plays cricketer Sandeep Patil?
104. Which is the only Asian country to be located completely in the Southern Hemisphere?
105. The Kingdom of Denmark includes 2 self-governing territories. Greenland is one; which is the other?
106. Which author, with the same last name as an Indian Chief Minister, was born in Calcutta and then educated in England? His most famous work features the protagonist, Becky Sharp.

107. The 1904 Younghusband expedition was an invasion of which region, primarily to counter potential Russian advances towards British India?

108. Which play is considered by many thespians as *cursed*, with the belief that uttering the play's name inside a theater, other than as called for in the script while rehearsing or performing, will invite disaster?

109. Which poem, first published in *Lyrical Ballads* in 1798, was adapted into a 1984 song of the same name by the band *Iron Maiden*?

110. The travel book *A Walk in the Woods* is a chronicle of author Bill Bryson's hike along which 3,500km-long trail?

111. Multiple theories exist for the name. One states it is named after an old castle 'Tirkan'. Another says it was named by the Turkish leader Suleiman Pasha after the then capital of Persia. A third says it comes from the term 'te ranat', which means 'fallen material' and refers to the earth swept down by water from nearby mountains. Which European capital city?

112. What evolved from the author's impromptu story to the three Liddell sisters, on a boating trip up the Thames in 1862?

113. The 2022 Hindi-language web series *Rocket Boys* is based on the lives of which two Indian scientists?

114. Which science fiction book series was, according to its author, based on ideas in Edward Gibbon's *History of the Decline and Fall*

of the Roman Empire?

115. How do we better know the statesman and lawyer Marcus Tullius, known for his oratory skills? His last name (also the name he is commonly known as) means chickpea in Latin.

116. How do we better know *Midgard* from Norse mythology?

117. Carthage, the capital of the ancient Carthaginian civilization, is located in which present-day country?

118. Which author, an English Member of Parliament and future Catholic saint, was beheaded by Henry VIII for treason in 1535? His best-known work describes an island governed along strictly rational lines.

119. How do we better know the singer and actress Cherilyn Sarkisian?

120. Which former Commonwealth realm transitioned to a republic in November 2021, with Governor-General Sandra Mason becoming the first President?

121. In the 2010s, who is the only player other than Lionel Messi and Cristiano Ronaldo to have won the *Ballon d'Or* award?

122. Who created Father Brown, a short, shabby, umbrella-wielding Catholic priest with a talent for solving crimes?

123. What monument on the Mississippi river was completed in 1965 and opened to the public in 1967?

124. Which business executive's autobiography is called *Straight from the Gut?*

125. If Idris was the last king of Libya, which country was Faisal II the last king of?

126. *The Four Musketeers* was a title given to 4 French tennis players who dominated tennis in the 1920s and 1930s, with a combined 20 Grand Slam Singles titles and 23 Doubles titles. Three of them were Jean Borotra, Jacques Brugnon and Henri Cochet. Who was the fourth?

127. If Air India is the flagship airline of India, what is the equivalent in Spain?

128. If Bruce Lee is known as the key proponent of the martial art style *Jeet Kune Do*, what martial art style is Ip Man associated with?

129. Which Vietnam War veteran, and recipient of a Purple Heart and Bronze Star for Valor, has twice won the *Academy Award for Best Director*, both times for war-themed films?

130. Which actor, who acted in all three *The Lord of the Rings* films, was the only member of the cast to have met JRR Tolkien in person, and read *The Lord of the Rings* trilogy every year from its year of publication until his death?

131. Aamir Khan has starred in multiple Bollywood films with sports themes including *Lagaan* and *Dangal*. Which was his first sports themed film?

132. Which superhit Bollywood film featured the protagonist suffering from a rare form of cancer called *lymphosarcoma of the intestine*?

133. Which ancient king of Magadha, whose name meant 'One whose enemy is not yet born' imprisoned his father and usurped the throne?

134. What term from Neapolitan cuisine means 'with garlic and oil'?

135. Which capital city, the former capital of Free France from 1940 to 1942, is located on the north bank of the Congo River?

136. Which Richard Linklater film, filmed from 2002 to 2013, has a script which evolved over the duration of filming, and was nominated for six Academy awards, winning one?

137. Who was chosen to finish writing the *Wheel of Time* book series, when its author Robert Jordan died in 2007?

138. Which highly reactive metal with atomic number 56 gets its name from the Greek word for *heavy*?

139. Which US state finds reference in the 1510 work *The Adventures of Esplandian*, and is described as a remote land rich in gold and pearls, inhabited by black women living like Amazons, and filled with strange beasts and craggy rocks?

140. What one word connects a county in Northwest England, a fictional cat, and a British WWII pilot and philanthropist?

141. The flag of the country of Kosovo features a map of Kosovo, making it one of two countries to have its own map on its flag. Which European Union member is the other?

142. The Swedish say *omelette* and the Argentinians say *whiskey*. What do we say in English?

143. What structure, which stretches 5,614 km from Jimbour in Queensland to Nundroo in South

Australia, was designed to keep a particular species away from sheep flocks?

144. Which comic character made his first appearance in 1951, and lives in Wichita, Kansas with his parents and pet dog Ruff?

145. Which writer of detective fiction is best known for novels like *The Maltese Falcon* and *The Thin Man*?

146. Which river, which runs through ten countries, and with its drainage basin extending into nine more countries, originates in the Black Forest of Germany and passes through four capital cities before emptying into the Black Sea?

147. Which water body, located at the tectonic plate boundary between the African Plate and the Arabian Plate, is 304 m deep, with its surface 430 m below sea level?

148. In Hindu mythology it is Kamadeva, and in Roman mythology it is Cupid. Who is the equivalent in Greek mythology?

149. The megadiverse Galapagos Islands, known for the large number of endemic species studied by Darwin, lie 900 km west of the South American mainland. Which country are they a part of?

150. What was first established by the Maastricht Treaty in 1992, with the name formally adopted in Madrid in 1995?

151. Which international cricketer, named by his father after his favorite English football team, later represented his country in Bridge championships?

152. What head covering, first named in an 1882 play, shares a name with a Linux distribution?

153. What dish, first referenced in a 1st century AD collection of Latin recipes, is known in 'purportedly' its country of origin as *pain perdu*, reflecting its main ingredient?

154. In JRR Tolkien's *The Lord of the Rings*, which character, the future steward of Gondor, resists temptation to take the One Ring from Frodo?

155. Which Thomas Hardy novel describes the life and relationships of Bathsheba Everdene with her neighbor William Boldwood, the shepherd Gabriel Oak, and the soldier Sergeant Troy?

156. What word connects the North American usage of a common motor fuel and a song by the band *Audioslave*?

157. Who is the protagonist in Elisabetta Dami's chapter book series for children, set in a fictional version of Earth dominated by anthropomorphic mice, and living in New Mouse City on Mouse Island?

158. Which 1960s American TV series starred Bruce Lee in his first major adult role?

159. Which 2000 song by the band *U2* credits Salman Rushdie as a lyricist, as the words are taken from his 1999 book of the same name?

160. What one word connects a region in West Africa, a former British coin, and a type of rodent used in lab experiments?

161. In which country was the government of the first post-Independence President Kwame

Nkrumah overthrown by the Armed Forces in 'Operation Cold Chop' in 1966?

162. Which band primarily consists of four animated members: 2-D, Murdoc, Noodle and Russel?

163. The only man to sweep the diving events in consecutive Olympics, which diver famously won gold at the 1988 Olympics after striking his head against the board and suffering a concussion during the preliminaries?

164. Which country, named basis the main kind of trade that occurred on its shores, is the world's largest exporter of cocoa beans, which account for 28% of its GDP?

165. Which play, a farcical comedy in which the protagonists maintain fictitious personae to escape burdensome social obligations, was first performed in 1895 and is also called *A Trivial Comedy for Serious People*?

166. Which moon of Jupiter has over 400 known active volcanoes, and is considered the most geologically active object in the solar system?

167. Which US state, known for its panhandle which follows a different time zone from the rest of the state, is also known for its potatoes?

168. How do we know the 1,500 km long annual sled dog race from Anchorage to Nome?

169. If it is Inspector Lestrade in the *Sherlock Holmes* stories, who is it in the *Hercule Poirot* stories?

170. Who played Don Draper in the TV series *Mad Men*, winning a Golden Globe and a Primetime Emmy award for the same?

171. Who was the first Indian fast bowler to take more than 300 wickets in One Day Internationals?

172. Which airport was formerly known as Idlewild Airport and renamed in 1963, now being one of six airports serving the New York City area?

173. The only country located in all four cardinal hemispheres; it is also the only country to be found in the earliest time zone (just west of the International Date Line). Which country, formerly known as the Gilbert Islands and whose current name is a local pronunciation of its old name?

174. Which *Mortal Kombat* character leads the Black Dragon, a criminal organization, and is distinguished by his cybernetic eye? He is also the archenemy of Sonya Blade.

175. In the *Harry Potter* universe, which is the smallest unit of currency, with 29 such units equivalent to a Silver Sickle?

176. How do we better know *citrus hystrix*, which is native to Southeast Asia? Its fruit and leaves are commonly in the regional cuisine. The first word in its two-word name means infidel in a language not native to the region.

177. Which country, the first African republic to proclaim its independence, was settled by free black people from the United States? Its capital is named after a supportive US President.

178. Which traditional song & dance form, typically performed to the beat of an instrument called *dholki*, is very popular in the Indian state of

Maharashtra, and is performed by female performers wearing nine-yard-long sarees?

179. Which city, located at the confluence of the Rhone and Saone rivers, was the capital of the Gauls at the time of the Roman Empire, and is now known for its gastronomy as well as architectural landmarks?

180. What term, also the name of a rodent typically found in Tundra biomes, is used to describe a person who "unthinkingly joins a mass movement, especially a headlong rush to destruction"?

181. Which military leader, known for his distinctive eye patch, served as Chief of Staff of the Israel Defense Forces during the Suez Crisis, & as Defense Minister during the Six-Day War?

182. Which US state is named after an eponymous river, a tributary of the Mississippi, which in turn gets its name from the Dakota for 'cloudy water'?

183. What preserve is made from the juice and peel of citrus fruits boiled with sugar and water, the preferred fruit being the Spanish Seville orange. The character *Paddington Bear* is known for his love of this preserve and always carries it in his briefcase.

184. Which country, the only African nation with full democracy, has a flag with four bands, with red representing the struggle for freedom, green the ocean, yellow the new light of independence, and green the agriculture?

185. Which smartphone, released in 2003 and mockingly called a "Taco phone" due to its shape, was Nokia's failed attempt to combine features of a mobile phone and a handheld game system?

186. Which fictional character, later described as an Indian prince, was named after the Latin for 'no one' or 'nobody'?

187. Which self-obsessed Greek mythological character stared at his own reflection in a pool of water for most of his life, eventually dying? A flower bearing his name is believed to have sprung from the place of his death.

188. The word means 'cloud' or 'fog' in Latin, and examples include Eagle, Horsehead, Oyster and Cat's Eye. What am I talking about?

189. Which word, which can also mean 'to successfully travel along or over', comes from the Latin for 'the carrying on of business'?

190. Which brand, first introduced in 1912 by a company then known as National Biscuit Company, is available in over a hundred countries? Each unit has 45 calories.

191. Which brand, incorporated in Mumbai as *Mirc Electronics* in 1981, is primarily known for its range of televisions? Its ads typically featured a devil, with a tail and horns.

192. How do we know the small humans, who were paid in their favorite food cocoa beans for working in a 'factory', and loved mischief and practical jokes? In early editions of the novel, they were portrayed as black African pygmies

but in later editions they were white skinned to prevent overtones of slavery.

193. What one-word name connects the Greek name for Rameses II, a character in the *Watchmen* comic book series, and a sonnet by the poet PB Shelley?

194. What word connects a character from Greek mythology, a satellite of Saturn, a music streaming service and jewelry brand founded in Denmark?

195. Which islands were named by the explorer Ruy López de Villalobos in 1543, in honor of the future king of Spain? Eventually the entire country took the name.

196. Who were created when Professor Utonium accidently added Chemical X to a mixture of 'sugar, spice and everything nice', when he was trying to create the 'perfect little girl'?

197. What English word, meaning timid or lacking courage, is also the name of a Roman legionary in *Asterix and the Chieftain's Shield*?

198. Which iconic character was portrayed by Desmond Llewelyn, John Cleese, and Ben Whishaw on film?

199. What subspecies of the zebra, distinguished by stripes only on the front part of its body, was hunted to extinction in the late 19th century?

200. Who, with Baba Looey, a Mexican burro, played the role of a sheriff in the Old West?

201. Which brand of cereal got its name because a partner Henry Seymour found an encyclopedia article on a religious denomination, and

decided that the qualities described of integrity, purity and honesty fit the product as well?

202. Element 104 in the periodic table was the subject of a decades-long battle between Russian and American scientists over its name. The Russians named it kurchatovium. What was the American name, named after a famous early 20th century physicist (also the element's now accepted name)?

203. Which fictional country is the setting the Anthony Hope novels *The Prisoner of Zenda* and *Rupert of Hentzau*?

204. What is the last name of the fictional John, who was born in 1947, is of Native American and German descent, served in Vietnam (where he was captured and tortured), and suffered from PTSD on his return to the USA, leading to the events he is known for?

205. What one word connects the metallurgical process of converting sulphidic ores to oxides, a cooking method, and a form of humor involving insulting an individual?

206. Most likely named after Empress Catherine II of the Russian Empire who founded the city in 1783, the city's location at the tip of a peninsula has made it strategically very important. Which city, which was annexed by a neighboring country in 2014?

207. One of the Bantu languages, it has an estimated 200 million speakers. A significant portion of its vocabulary includes Arabic loanwords, including its name which comes

from the Arabic for *of the coast*. Which language?

208. Which story chronologically begins just before the time of the 1857 Indian War of Independence, and sees action in Agra, the Andaman Islands, and London, culminating in a boat chase on the Thames?

209. Which forest in Nottinghamshire, England, is known for its association with the legend of Robin Hood?

210. Which country's current name means *Holy Island* in Sanskrit?

Set 1 Answers

1. The Code of Hammurabi, the code of law in ancient Mesopotamia
2. Leicester City winning the English Premier League in 2015-16
3. The Jetsons
4. They all lie on the mid-Atlantic Ridge
5. Cuban Missile Crisis
6. Belgrade
7. Aral Sea
8. Bonn, the former capital of West Germany
9. V for Vendetta
10. The Human Torch, in the Fantastic Four films
11. Riverdale from the Archie Comics universe
12. Mark Hamill
13. Robert Clive
14. Denmark. The town was originally called Tranquebar.
15. £10 per year
16. Lusofonia Games
17. Norway
18. Barbie
19. Satyajit Ray
20. Dara Singh
21. Galileo Galilei and Isaac Newton
22. Girish Karnad
23. The Beatles
24. Only Connect
25. Furlong
26. First siblings to win a doubles Grand Slam tournament

27. Giant Panda
28. Battle of Agincourt
29. Octavian
30. Damodar
31. Grotesque
32. Boston (Marathon)
33. Mozambique
34. Gerard Kuiper (Kuiper Belt)
35. Haiti
36. Weimar
37. George Gallup
38. Cobalt (from Kobold)
39. Boxing
40. Springbok
41. Kishore Kumar
42. Jet lag
43. Mirinda
44. 7 Up
45. Mountain Dew
46. Zamzam Cola
47. Ring structure of benzene
48. Citius, Altius, Fortius – the Olympic motto
49. Flora
50. Bankrupt
51. King George VI
52. Dr. BR Ambedkar
53. Purna Swaraj (Complete Independence)
54. Rajpath (formerly Kingsway)
55. Dr. APJ Abdul Kalam
56. Asp / ASP
57. Queen
58. Rasputin

59. Panama
60. Musth
61. Daulatabad
62. Michael Jackson
63. Humayun
64. Jagadish Chandra Bose
65. Cinderella Man
66. Palestine
67. Rajendra Chola
68. Fiji
69. Andy Murray
70. Shanti Niketan
71. Joan of Arc
72. Marie Curie herself
73. Poland
74. Birbal
75. Mali
76. Named after former Indian Prime Ministers
77. Nasser Hussain
78. Jeff Bezos
79. Chris O'Neil
80. Mammootty
81. Bombay
82. Singapore Sling
83. Morocco
84. Sense and Sensibility, by Jane Austen
85. Chinese Taipei
86. Charles Dickens
87. Libra
88. Durand Line
89. Jamaica
90. Norway

91. 'The Scream' by Edvard Munch
92. Lake Placid
93. Ulysses by James Joyce
94. Volleyball
95. Baccarat
96. Rome
97. 12 years a slave
98. Delhi
99. Dwight Eisenhower
100. Freddie Mercury
101. Star Wars (A New Hope)
102. Stromboli
103. Chirag Patil, the son of Sandeep Patil
104. East Timor
105. Faroe Islands
106. William Thackeray. The novel is *Vanity Fair*.
107. Tibet
108. *Macbeth*
109. *Rime of the Ancient Mariner*
110. Appalachian Trail
111. Tirana, Albania
112. *Alice in Wonderland*. The story was about 10-year-old Alice Liddell falling down a rabbit hole.
113. Vikram Sarabhai and Homi Bhabha
114. *The Foundation* series by Isaac Asimov
115. Cicero
116. Earth
117. Tunisia
118. Sir Thomas More. The book is *Utopia*.
119. Cher

120. Barbados
121. Luka Modric, who won in 2018
122. GK Chesterton
123. St Louis Arch, or Gateway Arch
124. Jack Welch
125. Iraq
126. Rene Lacoste
127. Iberian Airlines
128. Wing Chun
129. Oliver Stone
130. Christopher Lee
131. *Anwal Number*
132. *Anand*
133. Ajatashatru
134. Aglio e olio / Aglio olio
135. Brazzaville
136. *Boyhood*
137. Brandon Sanderson
138. Barium
139. California
140. Cheshire
141. Cyprus
142. Cheese – prompt by photographers before taking a picture
143. Dingo fence
144. Dennis the Menace
145. Dashiell Hammett
146. Danube
147. Dead Sea
148. Eros
149. Ecuador
150. Euro (currency)

151. Sir Everton Weekes
152. Fedora
153. French Toast (pain perdu means 'lost bread', reflecting the use of stale bread)
154. Faramir
155. *Far from the Madding Crowd*
156. Gasoline
157. *Geronimo Stilton*
158. *The Green Hornet*
159. *Ground Beneath Her Feet*
160. Guinea
161. Ghana
162. Gorillaz
163. Greg Louganis
164. Ivory Coast
165. *The Importance of Being Earnest*
166. Io
167. Idaho
168. Iditarod
169. Inspector Japp
170. Jon Hamm
171. Javagal Srinath
172. JFK (John F Kennedy)
173. Kiribati
174. Kano
175. Bronze Knut
176. Kaffir Lime
177. Liberia. The capital is Monrovia, named after James Monroe.
178. Laavani
179. Lyon
180. Lemming

181. Moshe Dayan
182. Minnesota
183. Marmalade
184. Mauritius
185. N-Gage
186. Captain Nemo
187. Narcissus
188. Nebula
189. Negotiate
190. Oreo
191. Onida
192. Oompa-Loompas
193. Ozymandias
194. Pandora
195. Philippines
196. Powerpuff Girls
197. Pusillanimous
198. Q from James Bond
199. Quagga
200. Quick Draw McGraw
201. Quaker Oats
202. Rutherfordium
203. Ruritania
204. Rambo
205. Roast
206. Sevastopol
207. Swahili
208. Sign of Four
209. Sherwood
210. Sri Lanka

SET 2: WEEKS 11-20

1. Who, also known as Lord Greystroke, made his first appearance in 1912, and subsequently in 23 sequels?
2. What form of High Intensity Interval Training involves 20 seconds of ultra-intense exercise followed by 10 seconds of rest, repeated continuously for 8 cycles, and is named after a Japanese sports professor who pioneered the technique?
3. Which brand's iconic shape is believed to have been inspired by the Matterhorn, which also features on the packaging? An alternate story suggests the shape comes from a pyramid that dances formed at a show that the founder attended.
4. What word connects a Helen Hunt starring movie, a game requiring physical skill, and a ice cream lollipop brand owned by Unilever?
5. Which former Secretary-General of the United

Nations was the first non-Scandinavian to hold the position, and helped facilitate negotiations between Kennedy and Khrushchev to defuse the Cuban Missile Crisis?

6. What name connects characters in *The Little Mermaid* and *F.R.I.E.N.D.S.*, to a body of water in British Columbia and a former Bond girl?

7. Which Bank, established in 1919, became the fifth largest private sector bank in India in 2019, when Andhra Bank and Corporation Bank were merged into it?

8. Whose biography, titled *The Queen of Indian Pop*, was released in February 2022?

9. Which city, a major stopover port for ships on the Atlantic-Pacific route, saw a decline after the opening of the Panama Canal, before seeing an artistic and tourism resurgence at the end of the millennium?

10. Which country was formerly a part of the Spanish Empire, and called *La Austrialia del Espiritu Santo*? It was later divided by England and France as the New Hebrides, before achieving independence in 1980.

11. Which chemical element was named by its discoverer after a name for the Scandinavian goddess of beauty and fertility? The name was based on the wide range of colors found in the element's compounds.

12. Which Batman Comics character, portrayed by Kim Basinger in the 1989 *Batman* film, is a journalist based in Gotham City?

13. What conflict lasted from 1455 to 1487, and

served as one of the inspirations for George RR Martin's *A Song of Ice and Fire* book series?

14. Which Bollywood actress started her Hindi film career with the movies *C.I.D.* and *Pyaasa*?

15. What began when Harry, Albert, Sam, and Jack acquired a movie projector and began showing films in Pennsylvania and Ohio?

16. Which is the only US state formed by separating from a Confederate state? It was admitted to the Union in 1863.

17. After which mutant and key character in the series, are the X-Men named?

18. Which musical instrument's name comes from the Greek 'sound of wood'?

19. Which TV series revolves around FBI special agents Fox Mulder and Dana Scully?

20. Which company was founded in 1906 as *The Haloid Photographic Company*, manufacturing photographic equipment and paper? Its current name is derived from the Greek for 'dry writing'?

21. Which Chinese city, a key point on the Silk Road, is home to the famous Terracota Army World Heritage Site?

22. Which caldera, formed during a volcanic super-eruption 640,000 years ago, fuels over half of the world's geysers included Old Faithful?

23. Which river, the longest to flow entirely within one country, is spanned by the Three Gorges Dam, and locally known as Chang Jiang?

24. Who served as President of Pakistan at the

time of the 1971 war with India and the secession of Bangladesh?

25. Which country was formerly made up of two countries, a military-controlled north and a communist south, with the two merging in 1990 to form the current state?

26. *Acanthurus lineatus*, also called the lined surgeonfish, is also known by which other name, due to its distinctive stripes?

27. What term, evolved from the old Semitic for 'protrude', refers to multiple massive structures built in ancient Mesopotamia for the purposes of worship?

28. Which former kingdom was founded by Shaka in 1816, and extended from the Tugela River to the Pongola River along the Indian Ocean, until defeat to the British Empire in 1897?

29. Which fictional character, formerly the President of the Galaxy, had two heads and three arms, and piloted the spaceship *Heart of Gold* in the H2G2 series by Douglas Adams?

30. How do we better know the story of Blondie, Angel Eyes, and Tuco Benedicto Pacífico Juan Maria Ramirez?

31. Which country is believed to get its name from the Sanskrit for 'garland of islands', or the Sinhala for 'necklace islands'?

32. If Napoli retired the number 10 jersey in honor of Diego Maradona, in whose honor did AFC Ajax retire the number 14 jersey?

33. In Plato's Republic, he references a mythical 'Ring of Gyges' which grants the user a special

power. Plato speculates whether a person would behave justly while wearing the Ring, because one's fear of earning a bad reputation would go away. Which science fiction novel from the 19th century is inspired by this story?

34. If the Academy Award statue is called an Oscar, what is the Dashiell Hammett Award statue, given in the field of crime writing, called?

35. What was first verifiably spotted in the Crimea in 1347, and travelled on Genoese ships across the Mediterranean to the rest of Europe and North Africa, lasting until 1353?

36. Antony Kamm played two matches for Middlesex in 1952. In 1960, he was asked to help translate a German novel to English and recommended his wife do it instead. The result was so well-received that she got to translate a major French series. What is the English world grateful for?

37. How do we better know Alexei Peshkov, who took as a pseudonym the local word for 'bitter', reflecting his anger about life in his country and his desire to speak about it?

38. If the Tyrannosaurus Rex was the primary antagonist in the first two *Jurassic Park* movies, which was the primary antagonist in *Jurassic Park III*?

39. Which award-winning American TV series, which ran for eight seasons, is based on the Israeli series *Prisoners of War*?

40. The Women's Cricket (50-over) World Cup,

has over its 11 editions, been won by either Australia (6 wins) or England (4 wins). The 2022 edition's final will be played between Australia and England again, so one of them will add to their titles. Which is the only other country to have won this tournament, doing so once?

41. What was the codename of India's 1984 mission to seize control of the Siachen Glacier in Kashmir, a name it shares with a Sanskrit poem written by Kalidasa?

42. Which English scientist attained fame for his planning and architectural surveys in the aftermath of the Great Fire of London? We better know him for the Law of Elasticity which bears his name.

43. Most moons of Uranus are named after characters from Shakespearean plays. Which is the only Uranian moon to be named after a character from Alexander Pope's *The Rape of the Lock*?

44. The iconic 1993 video game *Doom* is set on the moons of which planet of the solar system?

45. Which writer, born two weeks after the perihelion of Halley's Comet in 1835, wrote in his autobiography in 1909, that he expects to die when the comet appears again in 1910 (and he did)?

46. On which object in the solar system does the Isaac Asimov novel *Foundation and Earth*, the chronologically last *Foundation* series novel, end?

47. What new alphabet was invented in 1824, and based on a code that the French Army used to communicate at nighttime?

48. What nickname was given by newspaper reporters to the Hughes H-4 Hercules, the largest wooden airplane ever built in 1947? The name was a misnomer because the plane was made of birch.

49. What catapult type, which used a long arm to throw a projectile, is also the name of a commonly used font type?

50. The largest single muscle in the human body, it is also the name of the primary Roman character in *Asterix and the Olympic Games*. Name it.

51. Which animal gets its name from the Afrikaans for 'earth pig', because of its burrowing habits? It features on the top of most 'animal lists'.

52. Which snake, the sole member of the genus *Ophiophagus*, was for a long time classified in another genus due to physical similarities with snakes of that genus? In older literature, it was called a hamadryad.

53. In the Rudyard Kipling short story *Rikki-Tikki-Tavi*, the eponymous mongoose is helped by the animal Darzee when protecting his human family from snakes. What kind of animal is Darzee?

54. Which carnivorous mammal has a reputation for ferocity, with documented proof of killing prey many times its size? It is also a name of a very popular Marvel Comics character.

55. In *Asterix in Britain*, the chief of Anticlimax's tribe is named Mykingdomforanos, and is a caricature of Winston Churchill. Which Shakespearean play is his name inspired by?

56. In *Asterix and Cleopatra*, what future engineering work does Asterix hint at, after he has helped build the palace for Julius Caesar?

57. Dogmatix is the canine companion of Asterix and Obelix in many of their adventures. His name is, of course, a pun on *dogmatic*. What is his name in the original French comics, also a pun on a similar theme?

58. In *Asterix and the Actress*, what is the name of the Roman who drives the actress Latraviata to the Gaulish village? He drives recklessly and bears a resemblance to a Hollywood action hero if that helps.

59. Which personality, who died on 8-Apr, has his work typically divided into the Blue, Rose, and African-influenced periods? Two later periods are related to a style he co-founded.

60. On the second voyage of the HMS Beagle, famous for Charles Darwin's travels and research, what was the only location in Asia (now, technically, a part of Australia) that the ship passed through?

61. What event, the world's oldest of its kind, is traditionally held on Patriots' Day every year?

62. Six Space Shuttles have been built to date but Enterprise never went to space. Of the 5 which did, four are named Challenger, Columbia, Discovery, and Endeavour. What is

the fifth?

63. Which city, first documented in 1193, saw its Jewish community wiped out in the Holocaust? A significant event 36 years ago led to the city's abandonment.

64. Which country's national anthem has different lyrics for each of the country's four official languages – German, French, Italian and Romansh?

65. Which country's anthem is considered the world's oldest, the words dating to the 10th century? It was set to music only in 1880 and continues to be named *His Imperial Majesty's Reign* even though the country is now a parliamentary democracy.

66. Which Nobel Laureate has penned the national anthems of two sovereign states, both of which are in the same language?

67. Which country's national anthem is called, in English, *Song of Abidjan*?

68. Which country, with four official languages, uses only one of them (the de facto national language) for its national anthem, despite it being a minority language in the country?

69. San Marino, Kosovo, and Bosnia and Herzogovina are three of four countries with national anthems sans official lyrics. Which is the fourth such country?

70. Which country's national anthem, titled in English *This is the Home of the Brave*, is sung a cappella, because musical instruments are prohibited for religious reasons?

71. Which country's anthem was written in 1792 after it declared war on Austria, and adopted as the official anthem in 1795?

72. Which entirely planned city, also the country's largest inland city, was chosen as capital in 1913 (and then built) as a compromise between the country's two largest cities? It is popularly believed that its name comes from the Indigenous word for 'meeting place'.

73. What city, at the time ruined and uninhabited, was made capital of the newly independent country in 1834, with the romantic notion of reviving the country's ancient glory?

74. What common name is shared by the capital cities of Guyana, Cayman Islands and Ascension Island?

75. Which capital city got its name in the 3rd century AD because it was in the region of three cities – Oea, Sabratha and Leptis Magna?

76. Which capital city is located at the confluence of the White Nile and Blue Nile rivers, and consequently divided into three parts by the two and the Nile River they merge into?

77. Which city, originally called Akmolinsk, became the new capital city of its country in 1997 and was renamed to mean 'capital city' in the local language? It was renamed again in 2019 in honor of the country's long-ruling President who resigned that year.

78. Which city, which gets its name from the Turkic for 'stone city', was the location of the untimely death of the Prime Minister of India

in 1966?

79. Which city in India, itself a Union Territory, serves as the capital of two states in India?

80. Which Soviet writer, best known for the novel *Doctor Zhivago*, won the Nobel Prize for Literature in 1958, but was forced by his government to reject it?

81. Which French philosopher, playwright and novelist refused the Literature Nobel Prize in 1964 as he did not want to accept any official honors for his work?

82. The 2021 Literature Nobel Prize winner Abdulrazak Gurnah's novels deal primarily with the effects of colonialism. Which country was he born in, before moving to the United Kingdom as a refugee?

83. Which novel by Turkish Literature Nobel Laureate Orhan Pamuk is also the name of a location in Istanbul? Visitors who bring a copy of the book are allowed free entry.

84. Which Literature Nobel Laureate, writing in Spanish, set many of his works in the fictional village of Macondo?

85. Which Indian-born author, known for novels such as *Such a Long Journey* and *A Fine Balance*, explores themes in Parsi life?

86. Which Man Booker prize winning Indian author is in turn the daughter of a three-time Booker nominated author?

87. Which writer, best known for his fiction, has also written *What I Talk About When I Talk About Running*, a series of essays about his

experience as a marathon runner?

88. Which English novelist wrote *The Moonstone*, considered by many as the first modern English detective novel?

89. Which popular singer and Grammy award winner appeared in a cameo on the show *Game of Thrones* in 2017?

90. Which billionaire and entrepreneur launched his first business venture at the age of 16, by starting a magazine called *Student*?

91. Which actor and comedian is known for his passion for lemurs, having hosted a documentary on lemurs, as well as having the Bemaraha woolly lemur named after him? The ring-tailed lemur played a key role in his 1997 film *Fierce Creatures*.

92. Which American singer, known as the 'Demon of Screamin' for his vocal range, sang songs such as *Dream On* and *Sweet Emotion*?

93. Two countries have pegged their currency to the Indian rupee - Nepal and which other?

94. Which country's currency is named the bolivar, after Simon Bolivar, the hero of Latin American independence?

95. Which country's currency is called the togrog, from the local word for 'circular object' or coin, and was originally pegged to the Soviet ruble in 1925?

96. Which country, the world's smallest republic and with an environment damaged by phosphate mining, uses the Australian dollar as its currency, signifying its heavy dependence

on Australia for everything?

97. Which country's currency gets its name from the local word for gold – zloto?

98. Which country replaced the West African pound as its currency in 1964, the currency bearing the same name as the second word in the country's name?

99. Which country, a former part of the USSR, uses the 'dram' as its currency? Nothing, of course, to do with the scotch whisky drams.

100. Which Latin American country voted legislation to make Bitcoin legal tender in 2021? Given the volatility of Bitcoin, this has caused economic hardship in the country.

101. Which former President of his country, a shipyard electrician before his entry into politics, played a key role in his country's smooth transition to democracy, and won the Nobel Peace Prize in 1983?

102. Ellen Johnson Sirleaf, the first elected female head of state in Africa, won the 2011 Nobel Peace Prize for her efforts to bring women into the peacekeeping process in which country?

103. If Barack Obama was (as of 2022) the latest US President to win the Nobel Peace Prize, who was the first?

104. Anwar Sadat and Menachem Begin won the 1978 Nobel Peace Prize for negotiating peace between Egypt and Israel. What name is given to these Accords, which were finalized at the country retreat of the US President in

Maryland, USA?

105. Which Norwegian winner of the 1922 Nobel Peace Prize devised a passport for stateless people, which is now named after him?

106. According to legend, which Indian state capital was originally named after Lakshmana, the younger brother of Lord Rama, and was called Lakshmanapuri?

107. And which Indian state capital is named after an incarnation of Goddess Kali, whose temple is located on Bantony Hill in the city?

108. Which naval surveyor in the East India Company discovered a natural harbor and named it after Lord Cornwallis? The eventual town helped the British fight pirates on the high seas and was eventually named after the surveyor (last name should do).

109. Which city, a winter capital of its state, is named after the river that flows through the city?

110. Karl Liebenberg, Cyril Mitchley and Sachin Tendulkar were involved in what cricket first, at Kingsmead, Durban in November 1992?

111. If Russell Endean of South Africa was the first in Test cricket, who was the first in One Day cricket? What dubious distinction do they share?

112. What cricket first was achieved by Colin Cowdrey in July 1968 against Australia at Edgbaston?

113. What cricket first did Garry Sobers achieve while captaining Nottinghamshire in a county

game against Glamorgan during the 1968 season?

114. How do we better know the *Mimosa Pudica*, a perennial flowering plant of the pea/legume family Fabaceae, and which exhibits rapid leaf movement?

115. Which fictional character, named after the German word for 'terror', lives alone in his swamp until he is forced to leave by the encroachment of fairy tale creatures?

116. Which author, a Pulitzer Prize and Presidential Medal of Freedom winner, was known for her low profile and reclusive nature as much as for her two books released in 1960 and 2015?

117. Which reclusive former actress was known for her somber persona in movies like *Camille* and *Anna Christie*, as well as her extensive art collection?

118. Whose death triggered the 1976 Tiananmen incident, when large crowds gathered in Tiananmen Square to protest the removal of official displays of grief?

119. Which long-term dictator's death in 1970 was followed, in his country, by the Carnation Revolution four years later?

120. Which politician and dictator got his moniker due to his past as a physician, and his medical work during WWII?

121. Which ruler of his country from 1959 to 1990 was considered autocratic, but is positively viewed within his country due to his role in transforming the country into a developed

nation?

122.What phrase, popularly used in East Africa, came to the Western World in an award-winning 1994 movie? The trademark for the phrase was awarded to the studio in 2003, leading to controversy and a change.org petition in East Africa.

123.What Hawaiian word, used to refer to an expert in any field, became globally popular because of its use in the name of a food item in the Quentin Tarantino film *Pulp Fiction*?

124.What doll-like character, commonly seen in late 19th century and early 20th century children's books, was characterized by jet black skin, eyes rimmed in white, exaggerated red lips and frizzy hair, and is now considered racist and a slur towards black people?

125.What word, used to refer to an overly oppressive environment, is a shortened form of *The Chief Administration of Corrective Labor Camps and Colonies* in the local language?

126.What versatile fiber, known to have been used since the Indus Valley civilization, gets its name from the Sanskrit for 'twisted hair'?

127.Which alcoholic drink brand, whose name means 'Master of the Hunt' in the local language, was rumored in an Internet hoax to contain deer blood, thanks to its color and its logo?

128.Which privately held spirits company got its logo inspiration from an animal that lived in the rafters of its first distillery?

129. Which Hebridean island is known for its distilleries, which include Laphroaig, Lagavulin and Ardbeg, and has its identity protected by law?

130. Which liquor brand is owned by Mohan Meakin Ltd. and is known for its complete reliance on word-of-mouth marketing?

131. As of May 2022, there are four footballers to have scored two hat-tricks in the FIFA World Cup. Three – Sandor Kocsis, Gerd Muller and Just Fontaine scored both their hat-tricks in the same event. Who scored his two hat-tricks across two World Cups?

132. Which country has made it to the FIFA final event eight times, but has never made it past the first round?

133. The Colombian defender Andres Escobar was famously shot dead in his home country after the 1994 World Cup, supposedly in retaliation for an own goal he scored which led to Colombia's elimination. Against which team did he score the own goal?

134. Fabien Barthez, the French goalkeeper during their successful FIFA World Cup title win in 1998, conceded only two goals during the tournament. One was a penalty in the group stage vs. Denmark. The other was a goal against which team in the semi-final?

135. Which plant, commonly used as a garnish across cuisines, is also used by Roman legionaries in the *Asterix* comics to stuff their ears, to avoid singing to the Gaulish bard

Cacofonix?

136. *Cymbopogon nardus* is a perennial aromatic plant, an invasive species which is unpalatable even for bovines, rendering it a weed even on pastureland. It can be used to produce an oil, used widely for its insect-repelling properties. How do we commonly know the plant?

137. The *Cinnamomum tamala* tree is native to the Indian subcontinent and China and can grow to 20m tall. Its leaves have a clove-like aroma with a hint of pepper and are used in food and medicine. How do we know this better?

138. The herb *Artemisia dracunculus* is widely used as an aromatic culinary herb. What is its common name, also the last name of the last victim of the crystal balls in the Tintin comic The Seven Crystal Balls?

139. Lewis Hamilton (with 103 wins as of April 2022) is the most successful British Formula One driver of all time. Who comes in second with 31 victories? Interestingly, this guy quit F1 as reigning champion, and went and won the CART Indy series in his debut season.

140. Which F1 legend remains the most successful driver by win percentage (as of April 2022), having won 46% of his entered races for a total of 24 wins? For context, Michael Schumacher won 29.5% of the races he entered in.

141. Who became the youngest driver to win a F1 Grand Prix race (as of April 2022), doing so at the age of 18 years and 228 days at the 2016

Spanish Grand Prix?

142. The 2005 United States Grand Prix is known for only three teams (with Bridgestone tires) participating, while all other teams (with Michelin tires) pulled out. Indian driver Narain Karthikeyan won his only career points when he finished fourth. Who won the race?

143. Norman Pritchard represented 'India' at the 1900 Olympics and won two silver medals, becoming the first person born in Asia to participate in and win a medal at the Olympics. Who was the first person to win an individual Olympic medal for independent India at the Olympics?

144. Which English chemist and X-ray crystallographer is often credited with the discovery of the DNA double helix structure, for which Crick, Watson and Wilkins won the Medicine Nobel Prize in 1962?

145. The French Revolution is known for the storming of the Bastille on 14 July 1789. Which other country saw a revolution on 14 July 1958, ending the monarchy and establishing a republic which lasted ten years, until replaced by a dictatorship?

146. Which former cricket umpire has published a book titled *Finding the Gaps: Transferable Skills to Be the Best You Can Be*?

147. Which rock band was founded in New Delhi in 1990, is known for its fusion style, and for songs like *Kandisa*?

148. The Vivek Express is India's longest train

route, covering 4,273 km from Kanyakumari in Tamil Nadu to which other city?

149. The Indian Pacific Railway connects which two cities in an iconic journey across a continent?

150. Navapur town in India has a railway station uniquely located across two states. Trains which halt there will be half in each state. Which two states does Navapur railway station straddle?

151. Former British imperialist Cecil Rhodes famously planned a railway across the length of Africa, connecting Cairo in Egypt to which other city in a then British colony?

152. Which political party was launched in 1913 with the release of a newspaper of the same name? The party's name meant 'revolt' in Urdu, and the newspaper was published in Urdu and Gurmukhi scripts.

153. Whose death in 1988 was followed by a declaration of cease fire by both the Soviet Afghan government and the Mujahideen, as his funeral procession traversed the Khyber Pass from Peshawar, Pakistan to Jalalabad, Afghanistan?

154. Which '3rd party' is best known for winning 5 states in the 1968 US Presidential Election with former Alabama governor George Wallace as its Presidential nominee, running on a racial segregation platform?

155. Which political party, founded in 1954, has remained the pre-eminent party in Singapore

till date, winning 80% of all seats in all elections since 1965?

156. Which footballer, a former player for the Kansas City Wizards and Sporting Clube de Portugal, received his country's highest sporting honor in 2021, becoming the first footballer to do so?

157. Nicknamed 'Magnificent', she has won eight World Championship medals in her sport and served as a nominated member of the Rajya Sabha from 2016-22. Who, after whom the stretch of road leading to the National Games Village in Imphal is named?

158. Which sportsperson, who made his Bollywood debut with the 2013 movie *Rajdhani Express*, represented India in a record seven Olympic Games, winning a bronze in his second appearance?

159. Which Arjuna Awardee dominated the Indian swimming scene in the 1990s and early 2000s, and represented India at the 2000 Sydney Olympics?

160. Better known for his antagonistic role in a Steven Spielberg film, who played the character of Khan in the 1982 Richard Attenborough film *Gandhi*?

161. Which Bollywood character, a master criminal, aims to conquer India from his remote island, and when things go his way, is visibly 'pleased'?

162. Which character is the fictional nephew of the above character, and serves as an antagonist in

a 1994 comedy film? His most common threat is to play marbles with his victim's eyes.

163. How do we better know Hamid Ali Khan, known for his classic Bollywood dialogues like 'Mona Darling' and 'Lilly, don't be silly'?

164. Whose grave can be found south of Shwedagon Pagoda, in Yangon, Myanmar? The exact site was lost over the years but refound and a mausoleum built in the early 1990s.

165. Which poet, singer, and member of the '27 club' died in Paris? His grave site is one of the most visited locations at the Pere Lachaise cemetery.

166. The final showdown in which iconic movie takes place at the grave site of 'Arch Stanton'?

167. Who returns to life in the fictional graveyard of Little Hangleton, after using bone of the father, flesh of the servant, and blood of the enemy?

168. Which animated film by Studio Ghibli focuses on two siblings in war-torn Kobe, Japan?

169. Which polar explorer, known for being the first to achieve a feat on 14 December 1911, went missing at sea in 1928, while on a rescue mission in the Arctic?

170. Which aviation pioneer disappeared over the Pacific in 1937, while on an attempt to circumnavigate the globe along with navigator Fred Noonan?

171. Which fictional superhero was presumed lost at sea in 1945, & found & awakened 70 years

later?

172. On 17-Dec-1967, Harold Holt disappeared while swimming in heavy surf, and was not found in spite of one of the largest rescue missions in the country. What title did he hold, which made his disappearance so sensational?

173. Which cricketer got his nickname because his school coach felt he resembled local Brisbane basketball player Leroy Loggins?

174. If Shoaib Akhtar was the Rawalpindi Express, what was Umar Gul called?

175. Which former England fast bowler was called Pica?

176. If Allan Border was Captain Grumpy, which former Ashes captain was The Iron Duke?

177. Which folk hero and sometime deity in Polynesian mythology is known as a trickster, and was voiced by Dwayne Johnson in a 2016 animated film?

178. What form did Lord Vishnu take to seduce the asuras into sharing the nectar of immortality, after the devas and asuras together churned the ocean of milk?

179. Which animal, native to North America, is considered in Native American myths as a noble trickster? All of us are more likely to have seen this animal in a Warner Bros cartoon series.

180. Which English folklore character, a sprite or fairy, plays a key role as a prankster in a popular Shakespearean play?

181. Which royal, labeled Madame Deficit for her

extravagant spending which many believed led to her country's financial crisis, was executed in 1793 after being convicted of treason?

182. Which dictator became the first sitting head of state to be charged with war crimes and genocide in 1999?

183. Which politician, President of Peru from 1990 to 2000, and known for severely crippling the Shining Path insurgency, was sentenced to prison for embezzlement, murder and human rights violations?

184. Which kleptocrat and President of his country for 21 years was ousted in the People Power revolution, before escaping the country with the help of the United States? His son became President of the country in 2022.

185. Rukmini Devi Arundale, the first Indian woman to be nominated as a member to the Rajya Sabha, was a dancer and choreographer of which classical Indian dance form?

186. Which Indian dance form, closely associated with a particular state, is a portrayal of the dance of love of Lord Krishna with Radha and the cowherd damsels of Vrindavan?

187. Which dance form, which originated among Cubans and Puerto Ricans in New York in the 1960s, is also the name of a variety of sauces?

188. Which dance form, closely associated with the Andalusian region of Spain, was first recorded in 1774?

189. Which dance form gets its name from the German for 'to roll or revolve'?

190. How do we better know lateral epicondylitis, a painful condition with gradual onset of symptoms? The popular name is due to players of a particular sport being highly prone to it, though most people in India will remember it for afflicting a player from a different sport.
191. Which highly infectious disease was historically referred to as consumption, due to the weight loss associated with the disease?
192. The discovery of the transmission method of which disease was made in Secunderabad, India in 1897, earning the discoverer a 1902 Nobel Prize?
193. Which chronic condition gets its name from the Greek for 'to breathe hard'?
194. Which tennis player, also a table tennis World Champion in 1929, was the last British player to win a Wimbledon Men's Singles title (winning in 1936) until Andy Murray won in 2013?
195. Before the record-breaking trio of Roger Federer, Rafael Nadal, and Novak Djokovic, who held the record for most appearances in the finals of Grand Slam tournaments, reaching 19 and winning 8?
196. Serena Williams and which other player remain the only two players to have won 6 Grand Slam Singles tournaments without losing a single set?
197. Which tennis player retired after winning his last Grand Slam title in his final appearance on court, at the 2002 US Open?

198. Which stringed instrument, typically with 5 strings and a circular cavity, is closely associated with Bluegrass music?

199. Former child prodigy and Carnatic musician U Srinivas was known for his association with which stringed musical instrument?

200. The balalaika, a stringed instrument with a characteristic triangular wooden body below the fretted neck, originated in which country?

201. Which stringed instrument produces sound through a wheel rubbing against strings, with a hand crank turning the wheel?

202. Which term in the world of business derives from the Italian for 'broken bench', and is believed to have originated in Renaissance Italy?

203. Which word comes from the Old Norse words for 'house' and 'tiller of the soil'? Its present-day meaning is something very different.

204. Which word comes from the Greek for 'word making', and has now come to mean 'the imitation of a sound' in modern English?

205. Which term comes from the last name of the French Finance Minister during the Seven Years' War? Because of the Minister's austere economic policies, his name became synonymous with anything done or made cheaply, like outline portraits.

206. Which popular and instantly recognizable cartoon character, originally named Mortimer, debuted in 1928?

207. Which franchise, centered around an

anthropomorphic female animal, first aired as a TV show in 2004?

208. Originally a campfire song, it became hugely popular in 2016 when a South Korean company released a version of it on YouTube which went viral. Which children's song, featuring a lot of hand gestures?

209. Which animated TV series is set in the fictional kingdom of Dholakpur in rural India, and features a protagonist who shares his name with a key character from the Mahabharata?

210. Which Looney Tunes character is a large rooster with a Southern accent, and keeps humming the song "Everybody sing this song, doo daah"?

Set 2 Answers

1. Tarzan
2. Tabata
3. Toblerone
4. Twister
5. U Thant
6. Ursula
7. Union Bank of India
8. Usha Uthup
9. Valparaiso
10. Vanuatu
11. Vanadium
12. Vicki Vale
13. War of the Roses
14. Waheeda Rehman
15. Warner Bros.
16. West Virginia
17. Professor X / Charles Xavier
18. Xylophone
19. X-Files
20. Xerox
21. Xian
22. Yellowstone
23. Yangtze
24. Yahya Khan
25. Yemen
26. Zebra
27. Ziggurat
28. Zulu
29. Zaphod Beeblebrox
30. *The Good, The Bad and The Ugly*
31. Maldives

32. Johan Cruyff
33. *The Invisible Man* by HG Wells
34. The Thin Man
35. The 'Black Death' Plague
36. Anthea Bell, who translated the Asterix comics to English
37. Maxim Gorky
38. Spinosaurus
39. Homeland
40. New Zealand, in 2000
41. Meghdoot
42. Robert Hooke
43. Umbriel
44. Mars
45. Mark Twain
46. Earth's Moon
47. Braille
48. Spruce Goose
49. Trebuchet
50. Gluteus Maximus
51. Aardvark
52. King Cobra
53. Tailor Bird
54. Wolverine
55. Richard III (My kingdom for a horse)
56. Suez Canal
57. Idefix (Idee fixe)
58. Fastandfurious
59. Pablo Picasso
60. Cocos (Keeling) Islands
61. Boston Marathon
62. Atlantis

63. Chernobyl
64. Switzerland
65. Japan
66. Rabindranath Tagore. The countries are India and Bangladesh.
67. Ivory Coast
68. Singapore. The language is Malay.
69. Spain
70. Afghanistan
71. France
72. Canberra
73. Athens
74. Georgetown
75. Tripoli
76. Khartoum
77. Nur-Sultan in Kazakhstan, formerly called Astana
78. Tashkent
79. Chandigarh
80. Boris Pasternak
81. Jean-Paul Sartre
82. Tanzania
83. *The Museum of Innocence*
84. Gabriel Garcia Marquez
85. Rohinton Mistry
86. Kiran Desai
87. Haruki Murakami
88. Wilkie Collins
89. Ed Sheeran
90. Richard Branson
91. John Cleese
92. Steve Tyler

93. Bhutan
94. Venezuela
95. Mongolia
96. Nauru
97. Poland
98. Sierra Leone
99. Armenia
100. El Salvador
101. Lech Walesa
102. Liberia
103. Theodore Roosevelt
104. Camp David
105. Fritjof Nansen
106. Lucknow
107. Shimla, after Shyamala Mata
108. Archibald Blair (Port Blair)
109. Nagpur
110. First decision by a third umpire (Sachin was declared run out)
111. Mohinder Amarnath. Out handled the ball.
112. First player to play in 100 Test matches
113. Six sixes in an over
114. Touch me not
115. Shrek
116. Harper Lee
117. Greta Garbo
118. Zhou Enlai
119. Antonio Salazar
120. Papa Doc Duvalier
121. Lee Kuan Yew
122. Hakuna Matata
123. Kahuna

124. Golliwog
125. Gulag
126. Jute
127. Jagermeister
128. Bacardi
129. Islay
130. Old Monk
131. Gabriel Batistuta
132. Scotland
133. USA
134. Croatia
135. Parsley
136. Citronella
137. Indian bay leaf / Tej Patta
138. Tarragon
139. Nigel Mansell
140. Juan Manuel Fangio
141. Max Verstappen
142. Michael Schumacher
143. Kashaba Kadhav
144. Rosalind Franklin
145. Iraq
146. Simon Taufel
147. Indian Ocean
148. Dibrugarh, Assam
149. Sydney and Perth
150. Gujarat & Maharashtra
151. Cape Town
152. Ghadar
153. Khan Abdul Gaffar Khan
154. American Independent Party
155. People's Action Party

156. Sunil Chhetri
157. Mary Kom
158. Leander Paes
159. Nisha Millet
160. Amrish Puri
161. Mogambo
162. Crime Master Gogo
163. Ajit
164. Bahadur Shah Zafar
165. Jim Morrison
166. The Good, The Bad and the Ugly
167. Lord Voldemort
168. Grave of the Fireflies
169. Roald Amundsen
170. Amelia Earhart
171. Captain America
172. Prime Minister of Australia
173. Andrew Symonds (Roy)
174. Peshawar Rickshaw (Gul-dozer accepted)
175. Graham Dilley
176. Douglas Jardine
177. Maui
178. Mohini
179. Coyote
180. Puck
181. Marie Antoinette
182. Slobodan Milosevic
183. Alberto Fujimori
184. Ferdinand Marcos
185. Bharat Natyam
186. Manipuri
187. Salsa

188.Flamenco
189.Waltz
190.Tennis elbow
191.Tuberculosis
192.Malaria, by Ronald Ross
193.Asthma
194.Fred Perry
195.Ivan Lendl
196.Martina Navratilova
197.Pete Sampras
198.Banjo
199.Mandolin
200.Russia
201.Hurdy-gurdy
202.Bankrupt
203.Husband
204.Onomatopoeia
205.Silhouette
206.Mickey Mouse
207.Peppa Pig
208.Baby Shark
209.Chhota Bheem
210.Foghorn Leghorn

SET 3: WEEKS 21-30

1. Which kingdom was ruled by the Asaf Jahi dynasty from the early 18th century to 1947?

2. What came about in independent India because pre-Independence Gujarat consisted of three distinct parts – British-ruled Gujarat (a part of Bombay Presidency), the Gaekwad-ruled state, and a region comprising many princely states centered around Rajkot?

3. Which kingdom was last ruled by Palden Thondup Mangyal before its transition to democracy?

4. Which kingdom / princely state in India notably defeated the Dutch East India Company at the Battle of Colachel in 1741?

5. Which company was originally founded as Blue Ribbon Sports, and served as distributor for Onitsuka Tiger in the Western United States, before starting its own product range?

6. Which sportswear brand, now based in

Nottingham, England, was founded in Sydney in 1914, and uses a boomerang as its logo?

7. Which sports goods brand was started by brothers Harold and Wallace Humphreys, and uses a logo featuring two concentric diamonds?

8. Which sports company which now focuses on racquet sports, started in 1910 when it began making rubber golf balls as another line to its original business?

9. If Picasso's *Guernica* is based on the German bombing of Spain in the 1930s, then Goya's painting *The Third of May 1808* is based on Spanish resistance to whose armies?

10. Picasso is known for three anti-war paintings. *Guernica* is the first. The second is based on the Holocaust. His third anti-war painting, made in 1951, is based on which then active warzone?

11. Which phase of Picasso's work, characterized by somber hues, was influenced by his depression and by the suicide of his friend Carles Casagemas?

12. Which classic literary character's sketch, drawn by Picasso, was published in 1955, on the 350th anniversary of his first appearance?

13. Which mathematician and philosopher experienced three hallucinatory visions while serving as a soldier in Germany in 1619, that revealed a new system of philosophy to him?

14. Whose masterpiece on social contract was written during the English Civil War, and had copies burnt at the University of Oxford on

the charge of sedition, for its assertion that mankind is self-serving?

15. How do we better know the book *Being Memoirs of the Adventures of David Balfour in the Year 1751*, by an author who relocated to Samoa and came to be known as *Tusitala* (Teller of Tales) by the locals?

16. Which writer spent six years in Natal, South Africa and was deeply affected by the landscapes and myths he saw? It reflects in his best-selling adventure novels set in the region.

17. Who sang, among many other songs and jingles, the *Desh ki Dhadkan* jingle for the 1990s Hero Honda ad in India?

18. KK's first Bollywood song was as part of a quartet singing *Chhod Aaye Hum* in the movie *Maachis*. Which 1999 movie set in Rajasthan and Italy did he sing his first full song in?

19. Who composed the music for KK's debut solo album *Pal* in 1999?

20. Which label launched KK's debut album *Pal*? It was their first launch in the India market.

21. KK was nominated six times for the Best Male Playback Singer award at the Filmfare awards, but never won. He did win a Screen Award in 2009. For which song did he win, from the movie *Bachna Ae Haseeno*?

22. What parachute jumping technique is also the name of a popular video game franchise?

23. Which hugely successful video game featured powerups such as the Super Mushroom, Fire Flower, and Starman?

24. Which open-world video game franchise has seen its titles set in past versions of places like Florence, Rome, Istanbul, Boston, Paris and Athens?

25. Which 1993 first-person shooter video game was adapted into a 2005 film starring Dwayne Johnson, Karl Urban and Rosamund Pike?

26. Which country saw the long-term dictator resigning after the People Power Revolution, a series of non-violent demonstrations, in 1986?

27. Which country saw the toppling of King Farouk in the 23 July Revolution in 1952, leading to a period of only four Presidents over almost 60 years?

28. Which country, after its Revolution in 1989, tried and executed the former dictator and his wife? These remain the last people to be executed in the country, since capital punishment was abolished in the democracy that followed.

29. How do we better know the 1952-1960 war between the British colonial government and the KLFA (Kenya Land and Freedom Army), which the former won?

30. How do we better know Harald Gormsson, a king of Denmark & Norway from 958-986 AD?

31. Mehmed II, also called Fatih Sultan, ended the Byzantine Empire & took over Constantinople in 1453. What title was he known by?

32. George IV, King of the United Kingdom from 1820 to 1830, was known by what unflattering

title during his time as Crown Prince, due to his obesity?

33. Which ruler, called the 'Scourge of God', famously attacked both the Eastern and Western Roman Empires, and is known for his crossing of the Alps?

34. Which country, the smallest in mainland Africa, is situated on both sides of the lower reaches of the river valley of the same name?

35. Which Australian River, the third-longest in the country, shares its name with a term of endearment?

36. The longest of the rivers flowing into the Black Sea, which river originates in Germany, and was once the frontier of the Roman Empire?

37. Which Chilean River shares its name with the highest mountain in the Americas, even though its source is 20km away from the mountain, the latter lying completely in Argentina?

38. Mass production of what item began in the 1850s using the Bessemer process?

39. What innovation, credited with increasing production capacity drastically, was first seen in meat processing factories, but is most closely associated with Henry Ford?

40. What area of mathematics, first developed in its modern form by Newton and Leibniz, was also the name of a character in the English version of the Tintin comics?

41. What was first presented to the Russian Chemical Society in 1869?

42. What was first patented by George de Mestral in 1955, and popularized by NASA's use of it in space to secure devices in place?

43. Which Asterix story features characters such as Timandahaf, Riffraf, Nescaf and Epitaf?

44. Which anthropomorphic animal first appeared in a 1945 novel by EB White, and made his film debut in a 1999 film whose screenplay was written by M. Night Shyamalan?

45. Which English cricketer played for Surrey and Essex, had a highest Test score of 99*, and was nicknamed Bambi for his slender legs?

46. Which English dynasty began with the reign of Henry II in 1154, and ended with the death of Richard III in 1485?

47. Which plant has been cultivated for its edible seeds for over 3000 years, & is used primarily as a source of edible oil? It is also popularly known for its use in a phrase to unlock treasures.

48. Which ruler of the Abbasid Caliphate features prominently in the *Adventures of Sindbad the Sailor*?

49. Who wrote the fantasy novel *Two Years Eight Months and Twenty-Eight Nights*, set in New York City, and influenced by *The Arabian Nights*?

50. Which Indian television series, based on *The Arabian Nights*, ran from 1993-97 and was created by the Ramanand Sagar Group?

51. Which classic musical features the song "The rain in Spain stays mainly in the plain"?

52. Which musical features the protagonist being

called a flibbertigibbet, a clown and a will-o'-the-wisp by her superiors at the Abbey?

53. Which musical is set in the Ukrainian village of Anatevka, during the Tsarist Russia period and in the backdrop of the rising communist movement?

54. Which Best Picture Oscar winning musical is set primarily in Cook County Jail, and features the murder trials of its two protagonists?

55. Which marsupial, locally called the Thylacine, went extinct in the 1930s due to hunting, human encroachment, and introduction of dogs into its habitat?

56. Which now extinct flightless bird was endemic to New Zealand, and could reach 12 feet in height while weighing 500 pounds? It was hunted to extinction once humans settled the islands.

57. Which virus, at the center of a global eradication campaign since 1988, is now found in the wild only in the countries of Pakistan and Afghanistan?

58. In the 1993 film *Jurassic Park*, which creature's DNA is used to fill gaps in dinosaur DNA found preserved in prehistoric amber?

59. What unofficial accolade was given to the passenger liner in regular service, with the highest average speed across the Atlantic? The two-term term is also the name of an Indian brand of gin.

60. The Inca god Viracocha is believed to have been known by which other name, the latter

being adopted by a Norwegian explorer for a famous 1947 journey?

61. Which yacht, used in India's first circumnavigation in a sailboat, was displayed in a tableau during the 1987 Republic Day parade?

62. What type of ship, driven primarily by oars, was commonly used during the Classical period, and also depicted in the naval battle in the movie *Ben-Hur*?

63. Which novel tells the tale of Santiago, who goes to fish in the Gulf Stream off the coast of Cuba?

64. Which dam, built between 1931 and 1936, houses the Lake Mead reservoir, and has a different time zone at each end?

65. The Karababa Dam, located on the Euphrates River, was renamed after which leader who was the first President after the country transitioned into a republic?

66. Which dynasty built the Grand Anicut dam on the Kaveri River in the 2nd century AD? The dam is still in use and irrigates over a million hectares of land.

67. Which country would you find the Condor Cliff Dam in, on the Santa Cruz River? It was renamed after the country's President from 2003-07, who was in turn succeeded as President by his wife.

68. Which Ridley Scott film is an adaptation of a Philip K. Dick novel, and is set in a dystopian Los Angeles of 2019?

69. Which Ridley Scott film had its 'outdoor' scenes shot at Wadi Rum in Jordan, the latter being known for its red sandstone terrain?

70. Which Ridley Scott film won the 2000 Best Picture Oscar, also netting its lead actor the Best Male Actor Oscar?

71. Which Ridley Scott film is a fictionalized tale of the blacksmith Balian of Ibelin, and is set during the 12th century Crusades?

72. What title, first used during the Gupta Empire, did the king Hemu adopt when he ascended the throne of Delhi?

73. Which dynasty built the Kailasha Temple at Ellora, a cave temple built top down from a single rock?

74. Who started his military career with the conquest of Torna Fort at the age of 16, using the loot to build a new fort Rajgad?

75. Which dynasty is known for building the temple complexes at Belur and Halebidu in Karnataka?

76. Which bestselling novel follows the story and travels of the Andalusian shepherd named Santiago?

77. Which novel set during the North African campaign of World War II is a fictionalized tale of the Hungarian explorer Laszlo de Almasy?

78. Which science fiction novel is set on the desert planet of Arrakis, and focuses on Paul Atreides?

79. Which dark fantasy novel, the first in the *Dark*

Tower series, centers on Roland Deschain, who is chasing his adversary 'the man in black'?

80. The actor and director Sachin Pilgaonkar directed which popular TV comedy which starred his wife Supriya Pilgaonkar along with Reema Lagoo in the lead roles?

81. Which cricketer, named after the (more famous) Tendulkar, plays for Kerala in the Ranji Trophy and first appeared in the IPL for the Rajasthan Royals?

82. The music director Sachin Dev Burman won two Filmfare awards for Best Music Director, for the movie *Taxi Driver*, and which other movie which released in 1973?

83. Sachin was the name of a princely state in British India, and it lasted from 1791 to 1948. Which present-day Indian state was it a part of?

84. Sachin Nag is known for winning India its first gold medal at the 1951 Asian Games. He also competed at the 1948 Summer Olympics. Which sport did he primarily compete in?

85. Which Shakespearean play, adapted into a Bollywood film starring Sanjeev Kumar, is primarily set in the ancient Greek city of Ephesus (now in Turkey)?

86. Which Shakespearean play follows the King of Navarre and his three companions, as they focus on study and fasting after vowing to be away from women for three years?

87. The city of Verona in Italy is now, among other things, for being the setting for two plays

by Shakespeare. One of them is *The Two Gentlemen of Verona*. Which is the other?

88. Shakespeare's *Hamlet* is set in Denmark. Which of his plays is partly set in Egypt?

89. For 17 of the 50 US state capitals, the state capital is also the most populous city. Which is the only US state capital (named because of its view of a mountain range) to not feature in the top 20 most populated cities in its state?

90. 4 US state capitals have the word 'City' in their name. Oklahoma City (Oklahoma), Salt Lake City (Utah) and Jefferson City (Missouri) are 3. Which is the fourth?

91. Which US state capital was named in 1873 after a European head of state?

92. Which US state capital was named after a red colored pole which divided the hunting grounds of two Native American tribes?

93. What weapon, whose name meant 'long' in Arabic, was the preferred firearm of Pashtun warriors during the Anglo-Afghan wars? It also wounded Dr. Watson in the Sherlock Holmes series.

94. In the Sherlock Holmes novel *The Sign of Four*, in which city's fortress does the titular group of four come into being?

95. The 1962 Bollywood film *Bees Saal Baad* is based on which Sherlock Holmes story?

96. In *The Sign of Four*, after which territory not controlled by the British was Thaddeus Sholto's house named?

97. Brazil borders all other countries in mainland

South America save for two. Chile is one; which is the other?

98. What English word comes from the Quecha for dung? The quest for this item has impacted numerous avian populations across the globe.

99. Who captured and killed the Inca Emperor Atahualpa in 1533, setting the stage for the Spanish conquest and loot of the region?

100. Which country, the smallest in mainland South America, has descendants of migrants from India as its single largest ethnic group?

101. What emulsion, typically made with oil, egg yolk, and vinegar, is believed to get its name from Port Mahon in the Spanish island of Menorca, where it first originated?

102. What condiment, made using chili powder, glutinous rice, fermented soybean powder, barley malt powder, and salt, is traditionally naturally fermented in earthenware, sometimes over many years?

103. What food spread, dark brown in color, is made from leftover yeast extract from breweries, along with vegetable and spice additives, and was first developed in Melbourne in 1922?

104. What rhizome, first recorded in the 8th century AD, is used to make a pungent condiment known to stimulate the nose when eaten? The common version worldwide uses horseradish and food coloring.

105. What paste, native to the Maghreb region, derives from the Arabic word for 'to pound',

since it is made by pounding red chilies and adding spices such as garlic paste, caraway seeds, coriander seeds, cumin, and olive oil?

106. Which version of Android OS shared its name with the sister of Jughead Jones, from the Archie Comics franchise?

107. What dessert, typically made using biscuits, wafers, or cookies, was also the name of Android OS 4.0?

108. What confection, also the name of Android OS 4.4, was launched in 1935 as Rowntree's Chocolate Crisp, and got its current name after World War II?

109. What cookie brand, introduced in 1912, was also the name of the Android OS version released after *Nougat* and before *Pie*?

110. Which drummer, known for his destructive behavior including blowing up toilets with dynamite, died of an overdose of Heminevrin, a drug used to prevent alcohol withdrawal symptoms?

111. The band Led Zeppelin disbanded after their drummer John Bonham died in 1980. Who played drums at their reunion show in 1988?

112. Between drumming for Nirvana and Them Crooked Vultures, which band did Dave Grohl found?

113. For which band was Don Henley the drummer and lead co-vocalist?

114. What are people who have pogonophobia afraid of? The Gillette Company approves!

115. Some people fear particular colors.

Melanophobia is fear of black, and leucophobia is fear of the color white. If one has erythrophobia, which color do they fear?

116. What word, deriving from the Greek for 'marketplace', describes a fear for open spaces?

117. Equinophobia is not a fear of the equinox, as many would think. What is it a fear of?

118. Which city, the capital of its country, is the world's most populous Francophone city?

119. Which French speaking city on the river Rhone was the birthplace of the philosopher Jean-Jacques Rousseau?

120. Which city, a former Olympics host, is known for having the largest French-speaking population in the Western hemisphere?

121. Which country, which recognizes the President of France as a co-sovereign, uses Catalan and not French as an official language?

122. In which Steven Spielberg film did Audrey Hepburn make her final film appearance, in a cameo role as an angel?

123. We all know the film *The Martian* which focused on NASA's efforts to rescue Matt Damon's character from Mars. Which Steven Spielberg film involved rescuing a character portrayed by Matt Damon?

124. If *War of the Worlds* was a Steven Spielberg adaptation of an HG Wells novel, which of his films was an adaptation of a Philip K Dick novel?

125. During the filming of which movie did Steven Spielberg meet his future wife, Kate Capshaw?

126. In the Steven Spielberg film *Bridge of Spies*, which US fighter pilot's release is being negotiated, after his plane was shot down over the USSR?

127. What nickname did former Australian Test captain Allan Border acquire due to his dour demeanor during the 1989 Ashes, which he was determined to win (and did)?

128. Which batsman, in 2018, broke Allan Border's record of 153 consecutive Test appearances for his country?

129. At which ground did Allan Border take a match total of 11 wickets, his only ten-for in Tests? His total wickets tally in his career was only 39.

130. Allan Border led Australia to an underdog win at the 1987 Reliance World Cup, but he averaged only 22.87 with the bat during the tournament, with just one half century. Which team did he score it against?

131. In the film *Notting* Hill starring Hugh Grant and Julia Roberts, which artist's painting *La Mariee* features prominently in the story?

132. The Pointillism-style painting *A Sunday Afternoon on the Island of La Grande Jatte* by Georges Seurat, found in the Art Institute of Chicago, features in which 1986 classic set in the city?

133. The *Portrait of the Duke of Wellington* is a painting by the Spanish artist Francisco de Goya of the British general Arthur Wellesley, 1st Duke of Wellington, painted in 1812. It was stolen in

1961 (and later returned by the thief four years later). Which 1962 film, the first in a franchise, featured this painting, suggesting that the movie's villain was behind its theft?

134. In the 1999 film *The Thomas Crown Affair*, the protagonist steals which Impressionist's painting *San Giorgio Maggiore* at Dusk from the New York Metropolitan Museum of Art?

135. Herge's Tintin volume *King Ottokar's Sceptre* is purportedly based on the 1939 Italian invasion of Albania. The invasion of which region by Japan is the volume The Blue Lotus based on?

136. Which kingdom, considered the predecessor of the Czech Republic, was established in the 12th century, and became a part of the Austro-Hungarian Empire from 1867?

137. The 1938 Munich Agreement ceded which Czech territory to Nazi Germany?

138. Which country, occupied by Stalin and made a part of the USSR in 1940, got its independence in 1918, and had declared neutrality in 1939 (before its occupation)?

139. The 14th of July is known for Bastille Day and the French Revolution. In which country was the monarchy overthrown on 14-Jul-1958, paving the way for a republic?

140. Which chemist and philosopher who discovered oxygen was the primary target of rioters in Birmingham in 1791, purportedly for his support of the French Revolution?

141. Which novel begins with the release from imprisonment of the French doctor Alexandre

Manette, after spending 18 years in the Bastille prison?

142. Which king ruled France from 1830, after the Bourbon Restoration, till 1848 when he was overthrown, and the French Second Republic formed? His name inspired a popular Indian men's clothing brand.

143. Manitoulin Island is the largest lake island in the world, covering 2,766 square kilometers, and large enough to have lakes of its own. Which Great Lake is it found in?

144. A part of the most populous Muslim-majority country in the world, which island, with 149 million people, is the most populous island in the world?

145. Borneo is the largest island in Asia, and about 75% of its territory is occupied by Indonesia. Which two other countries have territory on this island?

146. Which fictional island, located in the North Sea, is where one would be sent if they cast an Unforgivable Curse?

147. What term, also the name of a fictional costumed crime fighter who operates from Bangalla, is used to describe an island which was included on maps for a period of time, but was later found not to exist?

148. Which acid, an essential nutrient commonly found in citrus fruits, helps treat scurvy? Also provide its common name.

149. Ethanoic acid (CH_3COOH) is most commonly found in which kitchen staple?

150. Named after the Latin for 'regal water', Aqua regia is named so because of its ability to dissolve gold. It contains which two constituent acids, in a molar ratio of 1:3?

151. Acid is the common street name for which psychedelic drug, whose full name is Lysergic Acid Diethylamide?

152. Who joined and was later removed from this list: Jacques Anquetil, Eddy Merckx, Bernard Hinault, Miguel Indurain?

153. The Tour de France traditionally ends in Paris. Which city did the 2022 edition start in?

154. What was unique about the Tour de France wins of Jean Robic in 1947 and Jan Janssen in 1968?

155. Which Asterix volume is based on the Tour de France, reflected in Asterix and Obelix journeying across Gaul, while carrying a yellow bag symbolizing the yellow jersey?

156. What measuring instrument, named after its 17th century French inventor, has to be adjusted for its zero-point error?

157. What measuring device, now seen in most vehicles, gets its name from the Greek for 'path' and 'measure'?

158. If a glucometer measures the concentration of glucose in blood, what does a sphygmomanometer measure?

159. What device, used to measure the angular distance between two visible objects, gets its name from the Latin for 'one sixth'?

160. Which Stanley Kubrick film is based on a

novel by William Makepeace Thackeray?

161. Stanley Kubrick collaborated with Kirk Douglas as lead actor in two films – one was *Spartacus*. Which was the other?

162. Stanley Kubrick's *Lolita* is based on Vladimir Nabokov's novel of the same name. Which of his films is based on a Stephen King novel?

163. For which film did Stanley Kubrick co-write the screenplay with Arthur C Clarke?

164. How do we better know the corner of Friedrich Strasse and Zimmer Strasse, which played a key role in moving between East and West Berlin during the Cold War?

165. What are the NATO phonetic codes for letters R & J, a reference to a classic tragedy?

166. In the NATO phonetic alphabet, Lima is named after a city, and Quebec after a province or state. Which letter is named after a country?

167. Which NATO phonetic code is also a month of the year?

168. Which NATO phonetic code is the name of a sport as well as a Volkswagen car model?

169. What began in 1978 after a debate between the Mid-Pacific Road Runners and the Waikiki Swim Club, about which athletes were more fit, runners or swimmers?

170. The annual Ironman World Championships are held in Kona, Hawaii. Where were they moved to in 2022 (the 2021 Championships) due to the Covid pandemic, a Utah city which sounds like it could slay a dragon?

171. In the first Ironman event in 1978, John Dunbar, a US Navy Seal, finished second. He had the chance to win, but his crew ran out of water in the run leg. What did they end up giving him?

172. Advance Publications, which owns the Ironman brand, pays royalties to whom to use the name?

173. Which city on the river Garonne hosts the world's main wine fair, Vinexpo, and is also home to companies such as Dassault Aviation?

174. Which region, which gets its name from the Latin for 'at the foot of the mountains', is known for the Barolo and Barbaresco wines?

175. The Marlborough wine region, at 41oS latitude, and known for its popular and eponymous Sauvignon Blanc, is found in which country?

176. Which region, flanked by the Mayacamas Mountain Range and the Vaca Mountains, came into prominence in the 1976 Paris Wine Tasting, when blind tasters placed its wine as superior to more well-known French brands?

177. For portraying American gold medal winning wrestler Dave Schulz in which movie, did Mark Ruffalo win an Oscar nomination for Best Supporting Actor?

178. Mark Ruffalo starred in the 2004 film *13 going on 30* opposite which actor??

179. In the 2010 film adaptation of which Dennis Lehane novel did Mark Ruffalo play a US Marshal, traveling with his partner to a hospital

for the criminally insane to investigate a disappearance?

180. In which 2013 heist film does Mark Ruffalo play an FBI Agent, alongside Jesse Eisenberg and Woody Harrelson, among others?

181. Which island country in the South Pacific, also known as 'The Rock', is one of the world's largest coral islands, and is a self-governing state under New Zealand?

182. Which island country in the Pacific has six major and over 900 small islands, and is best known for being the site of the World War II battle of Guadalcanal?

183. Which Pacific Island nation of more than 300 islands is known for its high percentage of people of Indian descent, and has mineral water as its largest export item?

184. Which Pacific Island nation, formerly called Pleasant Island, is the third smallest country in the world, has seen economic hardships since this phosphate reserves were exhausted in the 1990s?

185. Which Beatles song was written in March 1968 in Rishikesh, India, addressing the younger sister of actress Mia Farrow who sent a lot of time alone in meditation?

186. Which Beatles song was addressed to John Lennon's son Julian, right after Lennon's divorce? Paul McCartney eventually changed the name in the song from Jules to something else.

187. Which Beatles song is supposedly about Paul

and John taking a ferry to go to a town in the Isle of Wight in 1960? An alternate story narrated by John states that the song is named after what was given to the street cleaning of Hamburg once they established, they had a clean bill of health.

188. Which Beatles song is inspired by a Lewis Carroll poem, and features many psychedelic elements such as 'Sitting on a cornflake, waiting for the man to come'?

189. Which Beatles song was written by Paul McCartney in honor of his then girlfriend Jane Asher? It includes lines such as 'Bright are the stars that shine, dark is the sky'.

190. Which name of Lord Vishnu, appearing as the 650th name in the Vishnu sahasranama (1000 names of Vishnu), is also the first name of the protagonist of a science fiction series, which won a special Hugo Award for "Best All-Time Series" in 1966?

191. Which name of Lord Vishnu, appearing as the 48th name in the Vishnu sahasranama, means "He from whose navel comes the lotus", and is associated most popularly with a temple in Trivandrum?

192. Which name of Lord Vishnu, appearing as the 564th name in the Vishnu sahasranama, means "The resplendence of the sun", and is also the name of a former crown prince who is, as of 2022, a Member of Parliament in India?

193. Which name of Lord Vishnu, appearing as the 57th name in the Vishnu sahasranama, means

"He whose complexion is dark"?

194. Which Hanna Barbera animated character is a take on Snow White, as her guardian Sylvester Sneakly keeps trying to kill her for her inheritance, and the Ant Hill Mob of seven dwarf mobsters ends up rescuing her?

195. Which anthropomorphic Hanna Barbera character, voiced by Mel Blanc, is a spy designated Agent 000, who works for the International Sneaky Service?

196. Which Hanna Barbera character, an anthropomorphic canine, was known for his North Carolina Southern drawl, and his continuous singing of "Oh My Darling, Clementine"?

197. Which animated Hanna-Barbera family includes Fred, Wilma, Pebbles, and their friends Barney, Betty, and Bam-Bam?

198. Which company founded by two childhood friends in 1978, and known for its original ice cream flavors, was bought by Unilever in 2000?

199. Which Unilever antiperspirant brand was first developed in 1908 by Australian Samuel Fuller Sheffer and his wife, Alice? It was taken over by Unilever in 1989.

200. Which Unilever soap brand, established in 1931, gets its name from the Persian word for a public bathing establishment?

201. Which hair care brand, launched in 1947 by Godefroy Manufacturing, and then bought by Alberto Culver in 1968 and Unilever in 2010,

was originally marketed only to beauty salons?

202.King Richard I of England, known for his role in the Third Crusade, was known by what epithet due to his reputation as a great military leader?

203.Which Sultan's treaty with Richard I ended the Third Crusade? His tomb can be found in modern-day Damascus.

204.The fall of the Nasrid Kingdom in which Spanish city ended the *Reconquista*, the crusade to reconquer parts of Iberia ruled by Muslims?

205.The Northern Crusades, fought in the Baltic and Scandinavian regions, were called against which religious group?

206.Which castle with Tudor architecture, from the world of PG Wodehouse, is found in Shropshire, England, and is 2 miles away from the town of the same name, the latter having nine pubs?

207.Which country house, near Market Snodsbury in Worcestershire, is the home of the Travers family and best known for its gifted French cook Anatole?

208.Which gentleman's club in Dover Street, London, is frequented by Bertie Wooster? Its name describes the Edwardian stereotype of rich, idle young club members.

209.And which fictional club in Curzon Street, Mayfair, has Jeeves among its members? This club for valets and butlers has a two-word name, the second word also being the largest satellite in our solar system.

210. Which iconic luxury hotel in Piccadilly, one of the real locations in the Wodehouse universe, is frequented by Wooster and his family?

Set 3 Answers

1. Hyderabad
2. Three cricket teams in present-day Gujarat – Gujarat, Baroda, Saurashtra
3. Sikkim
4. Travancore
5. Nike
6. Speedo
7. Umbro
8. Dunlop
9. Napoleon
10. Korea
11. Blue Period
12. Don Quixote
13. Rene Descartes
14. Thomas Hobbes. The book is *Leviathan*.
15. *Kidnapped* by RL Stevenson
16. H. Rider Haggard
17. KK (RIP)
18. *Hum Dil De Chuke Sanam*
19. Leslie Lewis
20. Sony Music
21. *Khuda Jaane*
22. HALO
23. Mario Bros
24. Assassin's Creed
25. Doom
26. Philippines
27. Egypt
28. Romania
29. Mau Mau uprising
30. Bluetooth

31. The Conqueror
32. Prince of Whales
33. Attila the Hun
34. The Gambia
35. Darling River
36. Danube
37. Aconcagua
38. Steel
39. Assembly Line
40. Calculus
41. Periodic Table
42. Velcro
43. Asterix and the Normans
44. Stuart Little
45. Alex Tudor
46. Plantagenet
47. Sesame
48. Haroun al-Rashid
49. Salman Rushdie
50. Alif Laila
51. *My Fair Lady*
52. *The Sound of Music*
53. *Fiddler on the Roof*
54. *Chicago*
55. Tasmanian Tiger
56. Moa
57. Polio
58. Frog
59. Blue Riband
60. Kon-Tiki
61. Trishna
62. Galley

63. The Old Man and The Sea
64. Hoover Dam
65. Ataturk Dam
66. Chola
67. Argentina
68. Blade Runner
69. The Martian
70. Gladiator
71. Kingdom of Heaven
72. Vikramaditya
73. Rashtrakuta
74. Shivaji
75. Hoysala
76. *The Alchemist*, by Paulo Coelho
77. *The English Patient*, by Michael Ondaatje
78. *Dune*, by Frank Herbert
79. *The Gunslinger*, by Stephen King
80. *Tu Tu Main Main*
81. Sachin Baby
82. *Abhimaan*
83. Gujarat
84. Freestyle swimming
85. *A Comedy of Errors*
86. *Love's Labor Lost*
87. *Romeo and Juliet*
88. *Antony and Cleopatra*
89. Olympia, Washington
90. Carson City, Nevada
91. Bismarck, North Dakota
92. Baton Rouge, Louisiana
93. Jezail
94. Agra

95. *The Hound of the Baskervilles*
96. Pondicherry
97. Ecuador
98. Guano
99. Francisco Pizarro
100. Suriname
101. Mayonnaise
102. Gochujang
103. Vegemite
104. Wasabi
105. Harissa
106. Jellybean
107. Ice cream sandwich
108. Kit Kat
109. Oreo
110. Keith Moon
111. John's son Jason Bonham
112. Foo Fighters
113. The Eagles
114. Beards
115. Red
116. Agoraphobia
117. Horses
118. Kinshasa
119. Geneva
120. Montreal
121. Andorra
122. *Always*
123. *Saving Private Ryan*
124. *Minority Report*
125. *Indiana Jones and the Temple of Doom*
126. Gary Powers

127. Captain Grumpy
128. Sir Alastair Cook
129. Sydney
130. Zimbabwe
131. Marc Chagall
132. *Ferris Bueller's Day Off*
133. *Dr. No*
134. Claude Monet
135. Manchuria
136. Bohemia
137. Sudetenland
138. Estonia
139. Iraq
140. Joseph Priestley
141. A Tale of Two Cities
142. Louis Philippe
143. Huron
144. Java
145. Malaysia and Brunei
146. Azkaban
147. Phantom
148. Ascorbic acid / Vitamin C
149. Vinegar
150. Nitric acid and Hydrochloric acid
151. LSD
152. Lance Armstrong – five-time winners of the Tour de France
153. Copenhagen, Denmark
154. They did not win the yellow jersey until the last stage
155. *Asterix and the Banquet*
156. Vernier calliper

157. Odometer
158. Blood pressure
159. Sextant
160. *Barry Lyndon*
161. *Paths of Glory*
162. *The Shining*
163. *2001: A Space Odyssey*
164. Checkpoint Charlie
165. *Romeo and Juliet*
166. India
167. November
168. Golf
169. Ironman Triathlon
170. St. George
171. Beer
172. Marvel Entertainment
173. Bordeaux
174. Piedmont
175. New Zealand
176. Napa Valley
177. *Foxcatcher*
178. Jennifer Garner
179. *Shutter Island*
180. *Now You See Me*
181. Niue
182. Solomon Islands
183. Fiji
184. Nauru
185. *Dear Prudence*
186. *Hey Jude*
187. *Ticket to Ride*
188. *I am the Walrus*

189. *And I Love Her*
190. Hari
191. Padmanabha
192. Jyotiraditya
193. Krishna
194. Penelope Pitstop
195. Secret Squirrel
196. Huckleberry Hound
197. The Flintstones
198. Ben and Jerry's
199. Rexona
200. Hamam
201. TRESemme
202. Lionheart
203. Saladin
204. Granada
205. Pagans
206. Blandings
207. Brinkley Court
208. Drones
209. Junior Ganymede
210. Ritz

SET 4: WEEKS 31-40

1. Which fictional monkey with the ability to elongate his tail lives in the jungle of Kadu, and keeps saving his friends from enemies like Peelu the tiger and Dopaya the hunter?
2. Which fictional minister is always hatching plans to kill his trusting king and take over the kingdom, only for all the plans to backfire spectacularly?
3. Which fictional character, originally introduced in Tinkle comics as a village simpleton in 1983, is known for his stupidity?
4. Which enduring Tinkle comics character is known for always serendipitously saving the day, usually from man eaters? No one has seen his eyes yet.
5. Which game, published by Square Enix as the eleventh installment in a series, was the first console-based MMORPG, and is set in the world of Vana'diel?

6. Which MMORPG, released in 2004, is set in the world of Azeroth, and remains popular, with eight expansion packs released until 2020, and gaining over $9 billion in revenue by 2017?

7. Which MMORPG, while based on Norse mythology, was actually based on a Korean manhwa (comic) of the same name?

8. Which MMORPG, released on Windows in 2011, is set during a tenuous peace between the Galactic Republic and a re-emergent Sith Empire?

9. Which secret agent in the movie of the same name aims to recover a nuclear missile, with one of his colleagues and the princess of Salamia falling for him along the way?

10. Which movie has Cheenu protecting Viji, the latter having retrograde amnesia? The movie remains popular in both the original Tamil as well as Hindi – either name will do.

11. Kamal Haasan played ten roles in the movie Dasavathaaram. Which of these involved playing a real-life personality, who served as head of state of his country?

12. Which movie about the tragic love story of a Tamil man and a North Indian woman was Kamal Haasan's Bollywood debut in 1981?

13. Which polymath, known for his contributions to economics and Catholic canon law, is better remembered for his then radical astronomical model, published shortly before his death?

14. Which astronomer spent the last nine years of his life under house arrest, because he was

suspected of following the new astronomical model proposed by the person in the above question?

15. Which scientist, heavily influenced by the person in the above question, was born in the year that person died, is best remembered for his fundamental laws of classical mechanics?

16. Which astronomer, the second Astronomer Royal in Britain, helped fund the publication of the most famous book by the person in the above question? He is best remembered for a celestial body named after him, which can be seen from Earth at a well-known periodicity.

17. Which book, considered a classic of world history, is a collection of 196 letters written from prison and addressed by a father to his daughter?

18. Which book, whose English translation means 'My struggle', was written in prison after the author's failed 1923 coup?

19. Which satirical masterpiece was conceived by its author when he was in prison? The most prestigious literature prize in the author's country has been named after him.

20. *The House of the Dead* is a semi-autobiographical novel written by which Russian author, and based on his tenure in a Siberian prison camp?

21. Which French writer, known for his works involving sexual cruelty, wrote prolifically during a 11-year imprisonment in the Bastille?

22. The Kakori Train Conspiracy, a train robbery in 1925, was planned by Ram Prasad Bismil

and Ashfaqullah Khan, who belonged to which group? Its then name has the same initials as the typically largest component of salaries in India.

23. Which city in Uttar Pradesh, located 270 km from Delhi, was known for a 'Conspiracy' in which Ram Prasad Bismil led the sales of proscribed books, as well as looting to fund the same?

24. Which Indian freedom activist is known, among other things, for throwing the bomb in the 1912 attempted assassination of Viceroy Hardinge, in an event called the Delhi-Lahore Conspiracy? He fled to Japan and played a key role in Indian freedom activities during WWII.

25. With which country did Indian nationalist groups attempt to create a pan-British rebellion during WWI, with the eventual goal of launching a Mutiny in February 1915? The conspiracy was thwarted after British intelligence infiltrated the movement.

26. Which independence activist, who died of gunshot wounds during the Hindu-German Conspiracy in 1915, got his nickname due to his hand-to-hand defeat of a wild animal terrorizing his native village in 1906?

27. Which independence activist, portrayed on screen by Vicky Kaushal among others, assassinated Michael O'Dwyer as revenge for the Jallianwala Bagh massacre?

28. Which independence activist is best known for exploding bombs in the Central Legislative

Assembly in New Delhi in 1929, leading to his life imprisonment? He died in independent India in 1965.

29. Which independence activist & poet, known as Mahakavi, is best remembered for his patriotic songs and poems in the Tamil language?

30. Which princely state during the British Raj was part of the Bengal Presidency, and also lent its name to India's cricket tournament for under-19 players?

31. The Bombay Presidency of the British Raj had more than 350 princely states. Ruled by the 'Chhatrapati', which was the largest princely state by population in the Bombay Presidency?

32. Which princely state which attempted to secede to Pakistan, was annexed by India in November 1947?

33. Of the five 21-gun salute princely states in British India, two were ruled by Maratha clans. One was Baroda; which was the other?

34. What locations were renamed to Shaheed-Dweep and Swaraj-Dweep by Subhash Chandra Bose during the Second World War?

35. Which two Indian state capitals saw intense battles in 1944, and marked the furthest point of Japanese advance during the Second World War?

36. What did Winston Churchill refer to when he said, "if conditions are so bad, why has Gandhi not yet died of starvation"?

37. The call for the Quit India movement by Mahatma Gandhi came about at the All-India

Congress session in 1942, in which city?

38. Which future political leader started the 'Vanar Sena' (monkey brigade), a children's revolutionary group against British rule?

39. Which freedom fighter, later the first woman to be Chief Minister of an Indian state, played a key role in the Quit India movement, and sang *Vande Mataram* right before Nehru's famous *Tryst with Destiny* speech?

40. Which officer of the Indian National Army and Minister of Women's Affairs in the Azad Hind Government was also a trained gynecologist, and the sole opponent to APJ Abdul Kalam in the 2002 India Presidential elections?

41. Born in a Bengali family in Hyderabad, which poet worked as a suffragist in England before returning to India and joining the Indian National Congress?

42. Known for hoisting the Indian National flag at the Gowalia Tank maidan in Bombay during the Quit India Movement in 1942, which freedom fighter later became the first Mayor of Delhi, and was awarded the Bharat Ratna in 1997?

43. In the upcoming TV series, *The Lord of the Rings: The Rings of Power*, which future ringbearer and exile from Valinor will be played by Welsh actress Morfydd Clark?

44. From a *Lord of the Rings* mythology perspective, what connects Sauron, Isildur, Deagol, Gollum, Bilbo, and Frodo? Also finish the list.

45. In *The Hobbit*, what is Bilbo's official role in the dwarf expedition to the Lonely Mountain?

46. The Runic script in which Jules Verne novel is believed to have inspired JRR Tolkien's creation of the Dwarvish script?

47. Which country, geographically the closest to Antarctica, is only 350 km at its widest point east to west?

48. Penguins are found north of the Equator on a Pacific Ocean Island chain belonging to which country?

49. Which region, covering the Southern Andes and stretching to the Atlantic Coast, is also the name of an outdoor clothing brand?

50. Which region, mostly within Brazil but also extending into Paraguay and Bolivia, gets its name from the Portuguese for 'big wetland'?

51. The structure of which organic compound was determined by August Kekule after a dream in which a snake ate its own tail?

52. Which organic compound, a variation of which is found in aspirin, gets its name from the Latin for 'willow tree' and is used, like willow bark, to treat skin conditions like warts and acne?

53. Which organic compound, with the formula $CHCl_3$, is a colorless dense liquid, and formerly widely used as an anesthetic?

54. Which organic compound, a colorless flammable gas in its pure form, is widely used in the plastic industry?

55. Which is Salman Rushdie's first novel, written

in 1975 and based on the story of a Native American man called Flapping Eagle?

56. Which Rushdie novel won the Booker Prize as well as the 'Booker of Bookers', with the latter being awarded on the Booker Prize's 25th anniversary?

57. Which Rushdie novel gets its name from a song in the novel? The song lyrics were adapted by the band U2 and used in the 2000 film *The Million Dollar Hotel*.

58. Rushdie's 2019 novel *Quichotte* is inspired by a classic literary character created by which author?

59. In which African capital city, whose name means 'new flower' in Amharic, is the African Union headquartered?

60. Which country made Dodoma its official capital in 1996? However, due to design and planning delays, the old capital, whose name means 'Abode of Peace', still remains commercially most important.

61. This African capital city formerly became the capital of the Mossi Empire in 1441 and was named 'Wage sabre soba koumbem tenga', which means 'head war chief's village'. Which city, whose current name is a simplistic French rendition of the original name?

62. Which country, with two capitals at Mbabane and Lobamba, is the last absolute monarchy in Africa?

63. The city of N'Djamena, located on the Logone River as well as the country's border with

Cameroon, is the capital of which African country?

64. Which science fiction trilogy is set in a supercontinent called *The Stillness*, subject to frequent tectonic activities? All the 3 books in the series netted their author a Hugo prize.

65. Which science fiction novel, named after a classic orbital mechanics situation, is the first in a trilogy called *Remembrance of Earth's Past* in its English translation?

66. The *Space Trilogy* by which author is set on fictional versions of the planets Mars, Venus and Earth, called Malacandra, Perelandra and Thulcandra?

67. The *Sprawl* trilogy by William Gibson is best remembered for introducing words such as cyberspace and matrix. Which first novel in the trilogy begins in Chiba City, Japan?

68. Which British journalist was the inspiration for a character played by Meryl Streep in a 2006 Oscar nominated role?

69. Which women's lifestyle magazine has editions in over 60 countries? It was founded in Paris after World War II and its name is also a reference to women.

70. Which men's magazine shares its name with the first name of a popular Russian writer, who spent most of his life in exile until his return to the USSR after being personally invited back by Stalin?

71. The oldest women's English magazine in India, it has sponsored the Miss India beauty

pageant since 1964. Name it.

72. Literally meaning "one whose head is turned", this name was given to irregular soldiers in the Ottoman Army, recruited mostly from Albania and Circassia, and known for their bravery as well as brutality. What name?

73. A generic term for early European humans, it derives from 5 skeletons found by French paleontologist Louis Lartet at a rock shelter in Dordogne, France, while clearing land for a railway station?

74. Mammals of the order *Perissodactyla* digest plant cellulose in their intestines rather than their stomach, and include horses, asses, zebras, rhinos and tapirs. What English name do they go by, a literal translation of the order name? Something to do with their feet.

75. An early Germanic people, their name derived as a counter to a similar group of people from the east. Name this group which, under Alaric I, sacked Rome in 410 AD.

76. The smallest independent nation in the Caribbean Sea, it is 261 km^2 in area and includes two islands, giving it its two-part name. Name this country whose capital Basseterre is located on the larger island.

77. The second largest country in the Caribbean after Cuba, it declared independence from Spain only for its neighbor to annex it. It gained independence again 22 years later and has fought many wars with the neighbor since. Which country?

78. Which Caribbean nation, which transitioned from a Commonwealth realm to a republic in 2021, was ruled by the Spanish and then the Portuguese before being abandoned, and then taken over by England in the 1620s?

79. Which Caribbean nation of more than 3,000 islands is part of the Commonwealth with Queen Elizabeth II as head of state, and is known as a tax haven with its capital at Nassau?

80. Its name comes from the Italian for 'to cut off', referring to the method of stretching buffalo milk curds to form the cheese. It is typically served within a day of making and used a lot in pizza. Which cheese?

81. Which cheese is named after a town in North Holland, which in turn is known for its commercial cheese market since 1922? It is a semi-hard cheese typically sold in flat-ended spheres.

82. A Swiss cheese, it is yellow and medium-hard and was first mentioned in records in 1293. Historically, makers tried to avoid having holes in the cheese as they were considered imperfect, but now the holes are considered a sign of maturity. Which cheese?

83. Named after a town near Milan in Italy, this cheese is known for its sharp taste and blue veins and is eaten by Leopold Bloom in a sandwich in the 1922 novel *Ulysses*. Name it.

84. Which Egyptian cheese, hard with a pungent smell and made with no culture, gets its name

from the Arabic word for 'Roman'?

85. Serena Williams beat her sister Venus in the finals to win her first titles at the French, Wimbledon, and Australian Opens. Who did she beat in the 1999 US Open Final to win her first Grand Slam singles title?

86. Who did Serena Williams lose to in the semi-finals of the 2015 US Open, thwarting her attempt at a calendar year Grand Slam?

87. Serena Williams played her sister Venus eight times in Grand Slam singles finals matches, winning six and losing two. Who did she play the second most number of times, winning thrice and losing only once? The loss came at Wimbledon in 2004.

88. Which Belarusian player did Serena Williams partner in her two Mixed Doubles Grand Slam wins, both coming in 1998?

89. Which speech error, which indicates the misinterpretation of a phrase in a way that gives it a new meaning, was coined by the American writer Sylvia Wright in 1954?

90. Which speech error, in which two consonants or vowels are switched between two words in a phrase, is named after an Oxford don who reputedly used it a lot?

91. Which speech error, the mistaken use of an incorrect word in place of a word with a similar sound, is named after a character in Richard Brinsley Sheridan's 1775 play *The Rivals*? The character's name in turn comes from the French phrase 'poorly placed'.

92. Which speech error occurs due to the interference of an unconscious subdued wish or internal train of thought?

93. Which 1988 Studio Ghibli film tells the story of a professor's two young daughters and their interactions with friendly wood spirits?

94. Which 2006 Studio Ghibli film is based on a series of books by Ursula K. Le Guin?

95. Which 2013 Studio Ghibli film is a fictionalized tale of Jiro Horikoshi, who designed the Mitsubishi A5M and A6M Zero aircraft used by Japan in World War II?

96. Which 2013 Studio Ghibli film is based on *The Tale of the Bamboo Cutter*, a 10th century Japanese literary tale, and was nominated for the Best Animated Feature at the Academy Awards?

97. Which team sport, with players using only their feet, knees, shoulders, chest and head to touch the ball, uses a volleyball style court with a net?

98. Which Italian ball sport, similar to bowls, gets its name from the Italian word for 'bowl', and involves teams trying to get balls closest to a small ball called a 'jack'?

99. Which team sport has players on two teams, who try to throw balls and hit their opponents, while avoiding being hit themselves?

100. Which variation of football, in which players are allowed to run with the ball in addition to kicking it, is played between two teams of 18 players on an oval field?

101. Which Zimbabwean author became the first

Black African woman to appear on the Booker list twice, when her second novel *Glory* was nominated in 2022?

102. The 2022 Booker Prize shortlisted novel *The Seven Moons of Maali Almeida* is set in 1990, in a civil war in which country?

103. For which 2022 Booker Prize shortlisted novel did the author Percival Everett do extensive research on lynchings in the USA?

104. Which 2022 Booker Prize longlisted novel by Graeme Macrae Burnet shares its two-word name with a common teaching method at business schools?

105. Shortlisted for the 2022 Booker Prize for her novel *Oh William!*, which author is best known for her 2008 novel *Olive Kitteridge*, which was adapted into an Emmy-award winning miniseries starring Frances McDormand?

106. It was originally made using *Enhydris chinensis*, and likely brought to the US by Chinese railway laborers. It was considered beneficial due to high Omega-3 content. Later variants created by charlatans used specimens of the *Crotalinae* family, and often nothing at all. Now the term is synonymous with health care fraud. What two-word term?

107. Which one-time chairman of the NASDAQ stock exchange is known for running a $65 billion worth Ponzi scheme, until his 2008 arrest?

108. Which film by Steven Spielberg is based on the life of convicted fraud Frank Abagnale Jr., who

was played by Leonardo DiCaprio in the movie?

109. *Scam 1992*, based on a popular book by Sucheta Dalal, is based on which Indian stockbroker and his involvement in a securities scam?

110. The coat of arms of which European country features a golden eagle, an aurochs, a black eagle, a lion, and dolphins, each representing its different regions?

111. Which Commonwealth Realm country features a West Indian man and woman on its coat of arms, along with a crocodile on a log?

112. Which African country's coat of arms features a lion and a goat, both astride a shield with wavy lines, the lines representing a lake with the same name as the country?

113. Which city of dreaming spires has a blue lion, an elephant and a beaver on its coat of arms, with the centerpiece being the eponymous bovine on a body of water?

114. The body of water between South America and Antarctica is named after which explorer who circumnavigated the world in a single expedition from 1577 to 1580, and was second in command in the English victory over the Spanish Armada in 1588?

115. Which navigator and cartographer of the Ottoman Empire is best remembered for his *Kitab-i Bahriye* (Book of Navigation), which contains very accurate charts of the Mediterranean Sea and its ports and cities?

116. Which Portuguese navigator, in 1488, became the first European to round the southern tip of Africa into the Indian Ocean?

117. The Norwegian Viking explorer Erik the Red sailed to and settled in which region after being expelled from Iceland? His son Leif Erikson is believed to be the first European to reach the North American mainland when he reached Newfoundland.

118. Which quiz show started each episode with nine contestants, with players voting one contestant out after each round. The name of the show was what the voted out contestant was termed.

119. Which quiz show had individual contestants attempt ten questions, with content taken from elementary school textbooks?

120. If Bamber Gascoigne and Jeremy Paxman did it in the UK (Amol Rajan will be the third), who did it in India?

121. Which 1950s NBC quiz show was later found to be rigged, almost causing the TV quiz genre to end in the USA? It inspired the 1994 movie *Quiz Show*.

122. Roger Federer's first ATP tour final was at the 2000 Marseille Open, where he lost to a fellow countryman. Who?

123. Roger Federer's first big win was at the 2001 Wimbledon Championships, where he beat Pete Sampras in a five setter in the fourth round. Who did he lose to in the quarters, a local favorite who then went on to lose to the

final winner Goran Ivanisevic in the semifinals?

124. Who did Roger Federer partner to win the Men's Doubles gold medal in lawn tennis at the 2008 Beijing Olympics?

125. Roger Federer reached 31 Grand Slam singles finals and won 20. 6 of his losses were to Rafael Nadal, and 4 to Novak Djokovic. Who is the only other person to have beaten him in a final?

126. Roger Federer won his only French Open title in 2009, by defeating whom in the final?

127. What are sausages commonly called in the UK, due to their habit of often exploding because of shrinkage of the tight skin during cooking?

128. What sausage, originating from the Iberian Peninsula, gets its deep red color from dried and smoked red peppers? The Spanish and Portuguese versions are distinct, though the names sound similar. Give either name.

129. What German sausage gets its name from the Old German for 'finely chopped meat' and the German word for 'sausage', and sounds like the most ill-tempered child in a room?

130. Which country is known for *sai ua*, a grilled minced pork sausage flavored with curry paste and fresh herbs?

131. Ricardo Izecson dos Santos Leite won the Ballon d'Or in 2007, the last before the Ronaldo-Messi domination. How do we better know him?

132. Which national team captain won the FIFA

World Player of the Year and the Ballon d'Or in the same year, a rare feat for a defender but a well-deserved one, coming as it did in 2006?

133. Which midfielder, now a successful coach, won the 1998 Ballon d'Or while representing Juventus? One could argue that it wasn't his greatest achievement that year.

134. Who won the 1994 Ballon d'Or while playing for Barcelona, and also the Golden Boot at the 1994 FIFA World Cup?

135. Whose decluttering method features five steps, of which step three states "Keep only those things that spark joy"?

136. What secret to a happy life would one find at the convergence of what you love, what you're good at, what the world needs, and what you can be paid for?

137. What describes a mood of coziness and "comfortable conviviality" with feelings of wellness and contentment, a Danish word that was runner up to 'Brexit' as UK's word of the year in 2016?

138. *Friluftsliv*, or "free air life," is about embracing the great outdoors and your relationship with nature. Which country is this lifestyle associated with?

139. Fluid ejected by which mammal, known for other unpleasant properties, can cause temporary blindness if it gets in the eyes?

140. Which nocturnal primate has toxin-producing glands in its upper arms, which it then licks, making its bite poisonous to prey?

141. Which monotreme species is known for a venom gland on a spur of its hind leg, known to become active mainly during the mating season?

142. Variants such as the Northern short-tailed _____, Mediterranean water _____, and Eurasian water _____ are venomous insectivores with what common blanked out name? Something one would come across in a Shakespearean tale.

143. Which dramedy TV series starring Cybill Shepherd and Bruce Willis as private detectives ran from 1985 to 1989? The name of the show is in the news due to recent events in the Indian IT industry.

144. Which dramedy that ran from 1989 to 1993 and centered on a teen prodigy was remade in 2020 with a title character named Lahela Kameāloha (with the same nickname as the original)?

145. Which dramedy that ran from 1972 to 1983 was based on Richard Hooker's 1968 novel ____: *A Novel About Three Army Doctors*? The blank is the answer.

146. Which 1988-1993 comedy-drama series saw Fred Savage become, at 13, the youngest actor ever nominated as Outstanding Lead Actor for a Comedy Series?

147. Which 1979-1985 series centered on Bo and Luke, and their cousin Daisy and other family members, was remade into a 2005 film?

148. Which band formed in Lahore, Pakistan in

2002 originally featured Atif Aslam on vocals, and is best known for its song *Aadat*?

149. Which Danish-Norwegian dance-pop band was called Joyspeed when they formed in 1989, and is best remembered for the single *Barbie Girl*?

150. Which rock band that formed in Chicago in 1972 shares its name with a mythical river from Greek mythology, and is best remembered for songs such as *Lady* and *Come Sail Away*?

151. Which band, previously called *The Blue Velvets*, *Vision*, and *The Golliwogs*, took their three-word name in 1968? The final name came from a friend's name, an ad for the Olympia Brewing Company, and their renewed commitment to the band.

152. Which knight of King Arthur's round table is also a key figure in Welsh history and legend, and shares his name with an English cricketer born in Papua New Guinea?

153. Which knight of the round table is known for his doomed romance with Isolde (Iseult), and shares his name with a British volcanic island and archipelago in the south Atlantic Ocean?

154. Which knight of the round table is considered as the illegitimate son of Lancelot, and is renowned for his gallantry and purity as the most perfect of all knights, eventually succeeding in his quest for the Holy Grail?

155. Which knight of the round table is believed to have been leader of the Celtic Britons in

battles against Saxon invaders of Britain in the late 5th and early 6th centuries?

156. What is the common name of the berry, scientifically called *Atropa belladonna*, that is toxic when ingested, but belongs to the same family as tomatoes and eggplants?

157. Which berry also shares its name, in plural form, with a rock band formed in 1989 with Dolores O'Riordan as lead singer?

158. Which berry is poisonous in unripe form but edible when ripe? In the *Harry Potter* series, an artifact made using wood from the tree which bears the berries played a key role.

159. Botanically considered as a berry since each fruit is formed from the ovary of a single flower, which fruit is believed to have originated in Sudan, and can grow to over 90 kg in size?

160. Which Asterix character is named in sync with her husband, and is a seller one would never buy produce from, purely going by the two's names? In the French version she is *lelosubmarine*, a pun on 'Yellow Submarine'.

161. Which Asterix character, a cure for all illnesses, plays a key role in Asterix and Obelix joining the Roman legions to rescue her lover?

162. One of the few historical characters in the Asterix books, she likes to drink pearls dissolved in vinegar, and throws people who anger her to the crocodiles. Who?

163. Obelix's mother appears in *Asterix and the Actress* & is named after a spice derived from

an orchid species. She is *Gelatine* in the original. Name her.

164. The feathers of this bird have great cultural and spiritual value to American Indians in the US and are governed by the _____ feather law limiting the use of its feathers to certified and enrolled members of federally recognized Native American tribes. Which bird?

165. Brews from the feathers of which bird of the vulture family are used in traditional medicine in South America?

166. The feather of which bird is strongly associated with Lord Krishna, the eighth avatar of Lord Vishnu in Hindu mythology?

167. Which bird of the seaduck family has traditionally been hunted for its soft inner feathers, used in pillows and quilts? It has lent its name to the quilt type as well.

168. Many bird feathers have been used to fletch arrows. The last name Fletcher derives from this practice. What is the Swiss version of this name, shared by arguably one of the more famous people from that country?

169. In the 1990 film *The Hunt for Red October* starring Sean Connery, who played Jack Ryan?

170. Harrison Ford portrayed Jack Ryan in two movies – the 1992 film *Patriot Games*, and which movie in 1994, also the name of a doctrine adopted by the US Supreme Court to determine when limits can be placed on First Amendment freedoms?

171. The 2014 film *Jack Ryan: Shadow Recruit* starring

5Q Daily – The 2022 Collection

Chris Pine was an attempt to reboot the series. Who directed the film, while also serving as the main antagonist in it?

172. John Krasinski stars as the lead character in the television series *Tom Clancy's Jack Ryan*, making him the fifth actor to portray Jack Ryan on screen. Besides the names above, who else has played Jack Ryan, doing so in a 2002 film?

173. Which 1973 song was inspired by a red-headed bank clerk who flirted with the singer's husband, Carl Dean, at his local bank branch around the time they were newly married?

174. Which 1983 song was based by the singer on groupies he and his brothers encountered while they performed together, before he embarked on his solo career? No relation to the tennis star of the same name.

175. Which 1978 song was inspired by the prostitutes that the band's lead singer saw near the band's hotel in Paris, France, in October 1977? The song's title comes from the name of a character in the play *Cyrano de Bergerac*.

176. Which song, inspired by a love story that originated in 7th-century Arabia, was first recorded by Derek and the Dominoes in 1970, though it is more closely associated with one of the vocalists in the band?

177. Which species of rodent were the anthropomorphic duo Chip and Dale, created in 1943 by the Walt Disney Company?

178. Which Italian children's book series, published in English since 2004, is written by Elisabetta

Dami under the pen name of the title character, an anthropomorphic mouse who lives in New Mouse City?

179. Princess Sally Acorn, of the same species as Chip and Dale, is the primary love interest of which spiny mammal capable of running very fast?

180. The character Rat in *The Wind in the Willows* is actually what semi-aquatic rodent species?

181. Lake Titicaca, called the 'highest lake' in the world, is shared by Bolivia and which country?

182. Which lake is bordered by Kazakhstan, Russia, Azerbaijan, Turkmenistan, & Iran, and stretches nearly 1,200 kilometers north to south?

183. The freshwater lake Kivu is one of the African Great Lakes, and empties into the Ruzizi River, which flows into Lake Tanganyika. Rwanda and which other country share its waters?

184. Lake Constance, technically a part of the river Rhine, is at the conjunction of Germany, Austria and which other country?

185. The Laver Cup is an international indoor men's team tennis tournament played between Team Europe and Team World, annually since 2017. What court surface is it played on?

186. What is the women's equivalent of the Ryder Cup, a biennial men's golf competition between teams from Europe and the United States?

187. What tournament features three teams of 12 athletes (six men, six women) each from Team

Europe, Team US, and Team International, with one athlete from each team taking part in one of 12 match races over a 2km swim, 80km bike and 18km run?

188.At the 1992 Barcelona Summer Olympics, which team consisting of twelve of the fifteen former Soviet Union republics that chose to compete together, topped the medal charts with 45 golds and a total of 112 medals?

189.The West Indies is a multi-national cricket team representing the mainly English-speaking countries and territories in the Caribbean region and administered by Cricket West Indies. Which is the only constituent country to be part of a continental landmass, and is not an island?

190.Which Asian capital city was called Kaofu by the 7th century CE Chinese traveler Huen Tsang? Its current name was first applied to a river which empties into the Indus.

191.Which Asian capital city, formerly called Khuree, got its current name, meaning 'Red Hero', when it became the capital of a new socialist regime in 1924?

192.Which Asian capital city gets its name from the local word for 'mountain that brings happiness', a reference to its altitude of 800m in the shadow of the Ala-Too range?

193.Which Asian capital city was set up in 1769 as the new seat of administration, and witnessed a Japanese invasion in World War II, in spite of its European colonizer's neutrality in the war?

194. Which Egyptian pharaoh, the successor of Akhenaten, took the throne at the age of 9, and ruled until his death in his late teens? He is probably the best-known pharaoh across the world thanks to the 1922 discovery of his tomb.

195. The twelfth Peshwa of the Maratha Empire in India, he was the son of the assassinated Narayanrao Peshwa, and was installed on throne at the age of 40 days, ruling until his death in 1795 at the age of 21. Who?

196. Who became Queen of Spain at the age of three, ruling with the army's help until her abdication in 1870?

197. Which son of King Edward IV and de facto ruler of England was imprisoned in a tower along with his brother Richard of Shrewsbury, never to be seen again? His paternal uncle took over the throne as Richard III.

198. Which retail giant headquartered in Massy, France gets its name from the French word for 'crossroads', and employs over 300,000 people worldwide?

199. Which retail chain was started by Karl and Theo Albrecht in 1946 when they took over their mother's store in Essen, and split into two separate groups, one in the North and one in the South, in 1960?

200. Which home improvement retailer is headquartered in Mooresville, North Carolina, and opened its first store in 1921?

201. Which retail chain was started by Amancio

Ortega in 1975, and initially named after the 1964 film *Zorba the Greek*?

202. Conservation International identified 17 countries as 'Megadiverse' in 1998. Which megadiverse country is an island nation that was the setting for a successful 2005 animated film which launched a franchise?

203. Which megadiverse country, in 2008, was the first to legally recognize enforceable Rights of Nature, or ecosystem rights?

204. Which megadiverse country is the site of the Mount Kinabalu national park, a UNESCO World Heritage biodiversity site?

205. Which megadiverse country is known for its 63 National Parks, managed by the National Park Service?

206. Which British overseas territory is a volcanic island which was a key stopover for ships when they sailed from Asia to Europe via South Africa? It is better known as the location for the second exile of a defeated leader.

207. Which British overseas territory is the largest island in the Chagos archipelago, and saw a forcible expulsion of all inhabitants between 1968 and 1973 so it could be turned into a military base?

208. Which British island is known as the 'Queen of the Hebrides', and well known for its malt whisky distillation?

209. Which island, at the north side of Marguerite Bay off the west coast of the Antarctic Peninsula, is named after the wife of Queen

William IV, and thus shares its name with a South Australian city?

210. Which British overseas territory, formerly a base for privateers and now a tax haven, is also the name of a type of short trousers?

Set 4 Answers

1. Kapish
2. Tantri the Mantri
3. Suppandi
4. Shikari Shambhu
5. Final Fantasy XI
6. World of Warcraft
7. Ragnarok
8. Star Wars: The Old Republic
9. *Vikram*
10. *Moondram Pirai / Sadma*
11. George W. Bush
12. *Ek Duje Ke Liye*
13. Nicolaus Copernicus
14. Galileo Galilei
15. Isaac Newton
16. Edmund Halley
17. Glimpses of World History
18. Mein Kampf
19. Don Quixote
20. Fyodor Dostoevsky
21. Marquis de Sade
22. Hindustan Republican Association
23. Mainpuri
24. Rash Behari Bose
25. Germany
26. Bagha Jatin
27. Udham Singh
28. Batukeshwar Dutt
29. Subramanya Bharati
30. Cooch Behar
31. Kolhapur

32. Junagadh
33. Gwalior
34. Andaman and Nicobar Islands
35. Kohima and Imphal
36. Bengal Famine of 1943
37. Bombay
38. Indira Gandhi
39. Sucheta Kripalani
40. Lakshmi Sahgal
41. Sarojini Naidu
42. Aruna Asaf Ali
43. Galadriel
44. Characters who wielded the One Ring. Samwise is the last.
45. Burglar
46. Journey to the Center of the Earth
47. Chile
48. Ecuador
49. Patagonia
50. Pantanal
51. Benzene
52. Salicylic acid
53. Chloroform
54. Ethylene
55. *Grimus*
56. *Midnight's Children*
57. *The Ground Beneath Her Feet*
58. Miguel de Cervantes
59. Addis Ababa
60. Tanzania
61. Ouagadougou
62. Eswatini

63. Chad
64. *Broken Earth*
65. *The Three-Body Problem*
66. CS Lewis
67. *Neuromancer*
68. Anna Wintour
69. Elle
70. Maxim
71. Femina
72. Bashi-bazouk
73. Cro-Magnon
74. Odd-toed ungulate
75. Visigoths
76. St. Kitts and Nevis
77. Dominican Republic
78. Barbados
79. The Bahamas
80. Mozzarella
81. Edam
82. Emmenthal
83. Gorgonzola
84. Rumi
85. Martina Hingis
86. Roberta Vinci
87. Maria Sharapova
88. Max Mirnyi
89. Mondegreen, after 'laid him on the green'
90. Spoonerism, after William Spooner
91. Malapropism
92. Freudian slip
93. *My Neighbor Totoro*
94. *Tales from Earthsea*

95. *The Wind Rises*
96. *The Tale of the Princess Kaguya*
97. Sepak Takraw
98. Bocce
99. Dodgeball
100. Aussie Rules
101. NoViolet Bulawayo
102. Sri Lanka
103. *The Trees*
104. *Case Study*
105. Elizabeth Strout
106. Snake oil
107. Bernard Madoff
108. Catch Me If You Can
109. Harshad Mehta
110. Romania
111. Jamaica
112. Chad
113. Oxford
114. Sir Francis Drake
115. Piri Reis
116. Bartholomew Dias
117. Greenland
118. *Weakest Link*
119. *Are You Smarter Than a Fifth Grader?*
120. Siddhartha Basu – the host of *University Challenge*
121. *Twenty-One*
122. Marc Rosset
123. Tin Henman
124. Stanislas Wawrinka
125. Juan Martin del Potro, at the 2009 US

Open
126. Robin Soderling
127. Bangers
128. Chorizo / chouriço
129. Bratwurst
130. Thailand
131. Kaka
132. Fabio Cannavaro
133. Zinedine Zidane
134. Hristo Stoichkov
135. Marie Kondo
136. Ikigai
137. Hygge
138. Norway
139. Skunk
140. Slow Loris
141. Platypus
142. Shrew
143. Moonlighting
144. *Doogie Howser, MD*
145. *M*A*S*H*
146. *The Wonder Years*
147. *The Dukes of Hazzard*
148. Jal
149. Aqua
150. Styx
151. Creedence Clearwater Revival (CCR)
152. Geraint
153. Tristan
154. Galahad
155. Arthur himself
156. Deadly nightshade

157.Cranberry
158.Elderberry
159.Watermelon
160.Bacteria
161.Panacea
162.Cleopatra
163.Vanilla
164.Eagle
165.Condor
166.Peacock
167.Eider
168.Federer
169.Alec Baldwin
170.*Clear and Present Danger*
171.Kenneth Branagh
172.Ben Affleck
173.Jolene
174.Billie Jean
175.Roxanne
176.Layla
177.Chipmunk
178.Geronimo Stilton
179.Sonic the Hedgehog
180.Water vole
181.Peru
182.Caspian Sea
183.Democratic Republic of the Congo
184.Switzerland
185.Hard court
186.Solheim Cup
187.Collins Cup
188.Unified Team / CIS (Commonwealth of

Independent States)
189.Guyana
190.Kabul
191.Ulaanbaatar
192.Bishkek
193.Dili
194.King Tut
195.Madhavrao II
196.Isabella II
197.Edward V
198.Carrefour
199.Aldi
200.Lowe's
201.Zara
202.Madagascar
203.Ecuador
204.Malaysia
205.USA
206.Saint Helena
207.Diego Garcia
208.Islay
209.Adelaide
210.Bermuda

SET 5: WEEKS 41-50

1. Which vulture, the brother of Jatayu, provides directions to Hanuman's search party when they go south looking for Sita?

2. Which king, the younger brother of King Janaka of Mithila, saw his daughters Mandavi and Shrutakirti marry Rama's brothers Bharata and Shatrughna respectively?

3. Which demon and ruler of Patala carries away Rama and Lakshmana to the nether world, with the intent of sacrificing them, before he is killed by Hanuman?

4. Which servant of Kaikeyi convinces her to ask Dasharatha to send Rama to exile and put Kaikeyi's son Bharata on the throne?

5. Which tennis player, who won six Grand Slam singles titles, is the only player to have won the 'junior' singles Grand Slam, doing so in 1983?

6. Which tennis played completed two mixed doubles' Grand Slams in 1963 and 1965, before adding a women's Singles Grand Slam in 1969?

7. Which tennis player completed a singles Grand Slam and won an Olympic gold medal in the same year (1988), making it a Golden Slam?

8. Four women have won the women's doubles Grand Slam – Maria Bueno was the first in 1960 and was followed by Martina Navratilova and Pam Shriver (playing as a team in 1984). Who was the fourth player to achieve this feat in 1998?

9. Off the coast of which country did the naval battle of Trafalgar take place in 1805?

10. The 51-meter-high monument at the center of Trafalgar Square in London is named after which hero of the battle of Trafalgar?

11. Which country has donated the Christmas tree to Trafalgar Square since 1947, as a mark of thanks to Britain for their support during World War II?

12. There are four plinths at Trafalgar Square – one is empty and used for temporary artworks. Status of General Charles James Napier and Major-General Henry Havelock adorn two more plinths. Which king's statue adorns the last plinth?

13. What knife, which gets its name from an early 19th century pioneer and soldier, is known for its large size and cross guard, and is prominently seen in the Rambo and Crocodile

Dundee movies?

14. What knife, named after a town in Uttar Pradesh, India, has been seen prominently in Bollywood movies, with the blade typically concealed within the handle?

15. What knife, with a long slender blade and needle-like point, shares its name with a type of high heeled footwear?

16. What knife was designed to fit on the end of the muzzle of a rifle, allowing it to be used as a spear-like weapon?

17. Who was German Chancellor for only one night, after the previous holder of the position killed himself, and who followed the same example the next day?

18. Who was US President for only 32 days, dying in office in 1841, after delivering one of the longest (~ two hours) inaugural addresses in history?

19. Which Prime Minister of India stayed in office for only 170 days, making his the shortest total tenure of any Indian Prime Minister till date?

20. Pedro Lascurain served as the President for less than an hour in which country before he handed over power to General Huerta?

21. Prior to Liz Truss' short 45-day tenure as Prime Minister of the United Kingdom in 2022, George Canning held this record, with a 119-day tenure before his death from ill health. His son would go on to be Governor-General of India during which landmark event in the country's history?

22. The short story 'The Last Question' by which author brings in a science fiction element to the 'Let there be light' creation myth?

23. Bulbs with a tungsten filament were first demonstrated in 1904 by Alexander Just and Franjo Hanaman. What element did Thomas Edison use for his filament in his 1879 bulb?

24. The Elvish name of which High King of Lindon, portrayed by Benjamin Walker in the TV series *The Lord of the Rings: The Rings of Power*, means 'Star of Bright Light'?

25. Which scientist conducted experiments on the speed of light from 1877 until his death in 1931, coming up with a number of 299,796,000 m/s?

26. Diwali is referred to in the 7th century Sanskrit play *Nagananda* as *Dipapratipadotsava* (the first day of the light festival). To which Indian king is this play attributed?

27. Which Persian traveler, in his 11th century memoir on India, described Diwali as being celebrated on the day of the new moon in the month of Kartik?

28. The Portuguese traveler and trader Domingo Paes visited which Indian kingdom in 1520, and included a description of Diwali in his writings?

29. Which Mughal Emperor banned the celebration of Diwali in the year 1665?

30. In the US TV series *The Office*, the sixth episode of season three focuses on Diwali.

Michael Scott mistakenly believes Diwali to be an Indian version of what?

31. In which 2001 movie does Shah Rukh Khan run from a private plane to a helicopter, and then out of the helicopter to his waiting family, which is celebrating Diwali?

32. A young Vijay Khanna witnesses the murders of his parents on Diwali day in which film, which established Amitabh Bachchan as a superstar in India?

33. In which movie inspired by *Mrs. Doubtfire* does Kamal Hassan win a job as a governess after rescuing his daughter who is burnt by a firecracker?

34. Which Asura king, who features prominently in Assamese myths, is believed to have been killed by Krishna, with the victory celebrated on the day before Diwali?

35. Diwali is celebrated as the day that Rama, Lakshman, and Sita reach which location, after defeating Ravana and his army?

36. Which goddess is worshipped on Diwali, as it is considered the time she was born out of the churning of the ocean of milk by the devas and the asuras?

37. In Jainism, Diwali marks the day of the liberation of whose soul, the twenty fourth and last Jain Tirthankara?

38. CHOAM (Combine Honnete Ober Advancer Mercantiles) is a fictional business conglomerate in which science fiction universe,

most recently seen in a movie starring Timothée Chalamet and Oscar Isaac?

39. Which fictional corporation, falsely claimed to be an acronym for "A Company Making Everything", is commonly used by Wile E. Coyote in his attempts to catch the Road Runner?

40. Which fictional company started as an aerospace engineering firm in the Daily Planet building in Metropolis, before diversifying into a conglomerate, and serving as a front for its founder's nefarious activities?

41. Which fictional corporation is founded in 2099 by the merger of its parent British and Japanese corporations, and seeks to profit from a highly hostile extraterrestrial species?

42. Which fictional company is responsible for cloning the dinosaurs on fictional islands off the coast of Costa Rica?

43. With over 200,000 km of coastline, which country (inclusive of its constituent islands) has the world's longest coastline?

44. Which country, the smallest in mainland Africa, has a coastline which is almost the same as the mouth of the main river running through it?

45. If Ghana was the former Gold Coast, and Cote d'Ivoire was the former Ivory Coast, which country was the former Pepper Coast?

46. Which coastal region in Italy comprises the five villages of Monterosso al Mare, Vernazza, Corniglia, Manarola, and Riomaggiore, and

forms a UNESCO World Heritage Site on the Ligurian Sea?

47. Which Afghan city is believed to have been founded by Alexander the Great as Alexandria, before evolving to Iskandar and then over time to its current name?

48. Which Afghan city, a major center of Buddhism before the advent of Islam, is most closely associated with a dynasty founded by Subuktagin and expanded by his son Mahmud?

49. Which Afghan city, a key trade point between Kabul and Peshawar, served as the winter capital during the Durrani Empire?

50. Which Afghan city, a key location on the old Silk route and traditionally known for its wine, was a focal point of the Timurid Renaissance?

51. Which award did Khushwant Singh return to the government of India in 1984 to protest against Operation Blue Star?

52. Which popular magazine, that ceased publication in 1993, did Khushwant Singh run from 1969 to 1978?

53. Which 1956 novel by Khushwant Singh is set in 1947 and depicts the ground-level details of Partition?

54. Published in two volumes and covering a time period from 1469 to the present day, which people's history did Khushwant Singh first publish in 1963?

55. Which Enid Blyton character lives in Toyland, ferries toys around in his taxi, and counts Big Ears among his friends?

56. Which Enid Blyton series follows the protagonist Darrell Rivers and her adventures at a girls' boarding school?

57. There are three Enid Blyton series which feature children playing detective along with a canine friend – the Secret Seven is one, the Famous Five is another. Name the third.

58. Which Enid Blyton character is a naughty doll living in a room filled with toys, and was inspired by a handmade doll given to her on her third birthday?

59. Which Mexican city, considered the oldest still-inhabited city in the Americas, is known for its Great Pyramid, and shares its name with a hot sauce brand?

60. Which capital city, one of the oldest continuously inhabited cities in the world, served as the capital of the Umayyad Caliphate?

61. Which city in the West Bank is believed to have the oldest known protective wall, and shows evidence of occupation from 9000 BC? It is called the 'city of palm trees' in the Bible.

62. Which city was formerly known as Kashi and is a key center for Hindu pilgrimage?

63. Which city, called the 'world's greatest open-air museum', has been inhabited since ~2150 BC and gets its current name from the Arabic for 'palace'?

64. Which city, which became the capital of the Roman Empire in 324 AD, was called Nova Roma before it was renamed after the then

reigning emperor in 330 AD?

65. Which ancient city is considered the first of seven cities associated with the region of Delhi?

66. Saint Petersburg in Russia was renamed Petrograd in 1914, and then renamed again to what, in 1924? In 1991 it was again renamed to Saint Petersburg.

67. Which South African city's name was changed to Gqeberha, a Xhosa word used to refer to the Baakens River which flows through the city, in 2019?

68. Which Catholic priest and chess player wrote one of the earliest books on modern chess in 1561? The Spanish opening in chess is named after him.

69. The reigning champion Bobby Fischer forfeited the 1975 World chess championship against who, granting the latter the title?

70. Which chess champion went undefeated from 10 February 1916 to 21 March 1924, a period which included his 1921 World Championship victory over Emanuel Lasker?

71. 1948 was the first year FIDE hosted the World Chess championship. Who won the title that year, retaining it until 1963 except for a couple of years?

72. What term, that first emerged in the 1960s to describe how baby boomers were different from their parents, is now technically termed as "institutional age segregation"?

73. What measure of statistical dispersion used to

represent wealth inequality was first explained by an Italian statistician in 1912?

74. What term, used to describe the unequal access to technology, including smartphones, tablets, laptops, and the internet, came into prominence during the Covid-19 pandemic?

75. The concepts of First World, Second World and Third World countries emerged during the Cold War. What kind of populations are described as being part of a 'Fourth World'?

76. The exclave of Kaliningrad, formerly called Koenigsberg, is bordered by which country?

77. The Spanish exclave of Llivia is joined to Spain by a mile long road, and lies in which country?

78. The Dahagram–Angarpota exclave lies 200 meters within the territory of India, but belongs to which country?

79. The territory of Madha is an exclave of Oman within which country? Madha in turn has a second order enclave within it called Nahwa, which belongs to the country in question.

80. Where was the capital of Goa province of Portugal, before it was moved to Panaji in 1759?

81. Inscriptions dating to which dynasty are considered the oldest source of Panaji's name? The dynasty's name also features in Goa's state bus transport corporation.

82. What research institute, under the aegis of the Council of Scientific & Industrial Research (CSIR), in headquartered in Dona Paula, Panaji?

83. The 'Old Secretariat' building in Panaji, which housed the State Legislative Assembly until 2000, was built in the year 1500 as a summer capital by the ruler of which Sultanate?

84. The Kala Academy cultural center in Goa was designed in 1970 by which architect, also known for designing the Mahatma Gandhi Memorial at Sabarmati Ashram and the Madhya Pradesh Legislative Assembly in Bhopal?

85. Which science fiction novel by Pittacus Lore was adapted into a 2011 film starring Alex Pettyfer and Timothy Olyphant, among others?

86. What paradoxical situation, from which an individual cannot escape because of contradictory rules or limitations, forms the premise of a classic 1961 novel?

87. Which dystopian novel focuses on Winston Smith, a mid-level worker at the Ministry of Truth?

88. The title of which book, the second volume of a trilogy, refers to Orthanc and Minas Morgul?

89. Which Zimbabwean cricketer, whose last name is one of the many monikers of the Hindu God Lord Krishna, claimed Sachin Tendulkar as his only Test wicket in Delhi in 1993?

90. Which Bangladesh bowler, the first from his country to take 100 wickets in Test matches, claimed Sachin Tendulkar as his first scalp in Dhaka in 2000?

91. Which Australian all-rounder, known for his

captaincy skills, claimed Sachin Tendulkar as his first Test wicket in Bengaluru in 2008, when he toured as a leg-spinner and before his batting potential was realised?

92. Which later vilified cricketer took Sachin Tendulkar's wicket at Johannesburg in 1992? It was his first Test wicket, but definitely not the last time he dismissed Tendulkar.

93. What form of headgear, used to protect parts of the face, gets its name from a town which saw a significant battle during the 1854 Crimean war?

94. What headgear, typically associated with the Basque region, was once the national cap of France in its black form, and is associated with the military in its green form?

95. The Karakul hat is made with fur of the sheep breed of the same name, and originally comes from Bukhara. It has now fallen out of fashion in a country whose founding leader was known to wear it. Who?

96. What type of cap, typically worn when hunting a particular animal, is linked to detective work due to its association with a fictional detective?

97. The music for which movie, a 2010 sequel to the original 1982 science fiction film, was provided by the French music duo Daft Punk?

98. Which 1986 fantasy film, a cult success that spawned numerous sequels and TV spin-offs, had songs such as 'Who wants to live forever' and 'A kind of magic' by the band Queen in its soundtrack?

99. The 1969 movie *More* by Barbet Schroeder deals with drug addiction and is set in Paris and Ibiza. Which band, whose music style would be in sync with the subject matter, scored the music for the film?

100. Which 1999 film, based on a 1996 Chuck Palahniuk novel, features a soundtrack by the Dust Brothers?

101. Which flower, used in tea and also as a natural insecticide, originated in China but is more closely associated with the imperial seal of another East Asian country?

102. Which flower genus, with more than 300 known species, was closely associated with the Virgin Mary, and also symbolized the Houses of Lancaster and York?

103. Which flower species, scientifically called *Epigaea repens*, is the floral emblem of the US State of Massachusetts, where digging one up is punishable with a fine?

104. Which plant, known for its scented bell-shaped white flowers, is highly poisonous to humans, and hence features often in crime fiction, including a *Nancy Drew* novel and the TV show *Breaking Bad*?

105. Which spring-blooming flower which is found in multiple colors and has edible petals, is mostly closely associated with the Netherlands?

106. Which Indian scientist, who died on 21 November in 1970, is known for a phenomenon of light scattering which is

named after him?

107. Which Indian scientist, known primarily for his work with radio waves, also made contributions to botany and wrote science fiction in his native language?

108. Which Indian scientist, recipient of the Padma Vibhushan award in 2009, played a key role in India's nuclear tests and served as Director of the Bhabha Atomic Research Centre?

109. Which Indian scientist, who works mainly in solid-state and structural chemistry completed his PhD at the age of 24 and received the Bharat Ratna in 2013?

110. Which F1 racing driver from Finland won the 1982 F1 World Championship, a feat replicated by his son in 2016?

111. Which F1 racing driver was nicknamed the 'Flying Finn' and won 2 championships in 1998 and 1999?

112. Which F1 racing driver was nicknamed the Iceman and won the championship in 2007? He retired from the sport in 2021.

113. Which Finnish racing driver raced for Alfa Romeo in 2022, before previously driving with Williams and Mercedes?

114. Which former country did Argentina lose 1-6 to in the 1958 FIFA World Cup, for a bottom place finish in their group and thus an early exit?

115. Argentina won the 1978 FIFA World Cup at home but didn't go through the tournament undefeated. Against which eventual fourth-

place finisher did they lose 0-1 in a group game?

116. Argentina exited the 1994 FIFA World Cup in the Round of 16 with a loss against Romania. But who did they lose to in the group stage, in a match which Diego Maradona had to miss due to his doping ban?

117. Germany has beaten Argentina five times across the history of the FIFA World Cup (including matches played by West Germany). Which country comes next, with three wins against Argentina (as of 2022)?

118. Which country, which got its independence in 1975, made its sole appearance in the FIFA World Cup in 2006, drawing with Mexico and Iran, but losing a game with the country it was a former colony of?

119. Which country, in its only FIFA World Cup appearance till date, became the first Caribbean nation to reach the quarterfinals, doing so in 1938?

120. Which country, whose team is currently managed by Jean-Jacques Pierre, made their only FIFA World Cup appearance in 1974, losing their group games against Italy, Poland and Argentina?

121. Which country, which made its only appearance in the FIFA World Cup in 1970, won the AFC Asian Cup in 1964? Subsequent boycotts by other nations led to it now being part of UEFA.

122. Whose record of 180 ODI wickets did Jhulan

Goswami break in 2017, on her way to 255 wickets?

123. Jhulan Goswami took her career-best Test match figures of 10 for 78 at which ground, more famous for a Ganguly-Dravid partnership?

124. Anushka Sharma stars as Jhulan Goswami in which movie?

125. At which ground did Jhulan Goswami make her ODI debut, taking 2-15 against England in 2002?

126. Jhulan Goswami scored her only ODI half-century in Bengaluru in 2015 against which team, rescuing India from 52-5 to a total of 142, and enabling an India win by 17 runs?

127. Which team, then ranked 68th in the world and playing in their maiden World Cup, stunned reigning champions France in the 2002 FIFA World Cup?

128. Before Saudi Arabia beat them in 2022, Argentina lost the opening game of the 1990 World Cup to which team? This team's strong run to the quarters led to FIFA awarding an extra spot to African teams from the next edition of the World Cup.

129. Who, in a politically charged game, beat West Germany 1-0 at the 1974 World Cup? West Germany of course recovered to win the Cup that year.

130. In a match called the 'Miracle on Turf', which team, coming into the match with a 2-45 goal difference in their last seven matches, beat

England 1-0 at the 1950 World Cup?

131. The 1967 *Tom and Jerry* short called *The Mouse from H.U.N.G.E.R.* is a pun on which spy fiction TV series that aired from 1964 to 1968?

132. Which *Tom and Jerry* character, a middle-aged heavy-set African American woman, was removed from the series after 1953 due to protests from the NAACP?

133. Which 1944 *Tom and Jerry* short deals with a clothing style involving high-waisted, wide-legged, tight-cuffed, pegged trousers, and a long coat with wide lapels and wide padded shoulders? The 1943 Los Angeles riots targeted wearers of this style.

134. In the 1947 *Tom and Jerry* short Cat Concerto, Tom performs *Hungarian Rhapsody No. 2* by which composer of the Romantic period?

135. Shah Jahan commissioned the Taj Mahal as a mausoleum for his wife Mumtaz Mahal. On the banks of which river is it located?

136. The Shalimar Gardens, a garden complex which is now a UNESCO World Heritage Site, was commissioned by Shah Jahan in which city?

137. What item, later plundered by Nadir Shah of Persia in 1739 and then lost to history, was commissioned by Shah Jahan and located in the Diwan-i-Khas?

138. What structure, commissioned by Shah Jahan and completed in 1656, served as the imperial mosque of the Mughal emperors until the demise of the empire in 1857?

139. The title of which Pink Floyd album is derived from chapter seven of Kenneth Grahame's *The Wind in the Willows*, one of Syd Barrett's favorite books?

140. Which Pink Floyd album, released in 1976, had an image of the ageing Battersea Power Station on the album cover, over which was superimposed an image of a pig?

141. Which Pink Floyd album was adapted into a musical drama film starring Bob Geldof as the protagonist?

142. Which Pink Floyd album, whose cover features two large metal heads, each the height of a double-decker bus, in a field, had its name suggested by the writer Douglas Adams?

143. On 02-Dec-1982, retired dentist Barney Clark became the first recipient of what artificial item? He survived for 112 days after the procedure.

144. Which South African doctor, in 1967, became the first to successfully complete a human-to-human heart transplant operation?

145. What is the name of the phenomenon in which transplanted tissue is destroyed by the recipient's immune system?

146. The first successful transplant done in 1954 was a kidney transplant, which worked because of what criteria, that prevented severe immune reactions from the recipient's system?

147. In 2019, a patient in Maryland received a kidney transplant after spending many years on dialysis. What unique method was used to

deliver the donated kidney, a first in the history of organ transplants?

148. Which family band known for including Irish themes in their music comprises of siblings Jim, Sharon, Caroline, and Andrea?

149. Brothers Lester, Jules, Saul and Joe founded Modern Records in Los Angeles, and played a key role in the early years of rock and roll in the 1950s. What common last name did they share, indicating their Hungarian roots? You would be excused for thinking they are from an Indian state.

150. Which rock band formed in 1961 had an original lineup the consisted of brothers Brian, Dennis, and Carl Wilson, their cousin Mike Love, and friend Al Jardine? They are remembered for albums such as *Pet Sounds*.

151. Which band formed in 1969 consisted of brothers Duane and Gregg, with four others? They enjoyed success until Duane's death in a motorcycle accident at the age of 24, after which they have seen many periods of hiatus and reunions.

152. Which Bruce Springsteen song was written for a 1993 Academy-award winning movie, one of the first to portray gay people in a positive light?

153. What song by Don Henley is also a term used to indicate the higher pace of life on Manhattan Island, so that a standard unit of time passes by more quickly there?

154. What song by the band Queen shares its name

with a 1938 Graham Greene novel, both being set in an English seaside resort?

155. What song by Led Zeppelin was inspired during a drive through a desolate desert area of southern Morocco, with none of the band members actually having visited the place in the song name?

156. In the 2006 movie *Casino Royale*, what is the first drink that James Bond orders, after winning an Aston Martin DB5 in a bet in the Bahamas?

157. A 1962 bottle of which single malt does the villain Raoul Silva offer Bond, on an abandoned island off Macau in the movie *Skyfall*?

158. In the movie *Goldfinger*, what drink does James Bond have when he is a captive at Goldfinger's stud farm in Kentucky?

159. In *The Man with the Golden Gun*, the villain Scaramanga orders what drink, a cocktail of stout and champagne, that was first served in 1861 to mourn the death of Prince Albert?

160. The Côte d'Azur Airport is the third busiest in the country and serves which city, in addition to the nearby Principality of Monaco?

161. Resorts such as Dahab, Nuweiba, El Gouna and Marsa Alam (list not exhaustive) all lie on the 'Riviera' along which water body?

162. The cities of Ensenada, Acapulco and Salina Cruz form part of which 'Riviera', on the western coast of the country?

163. Which country's Riviera, called the Turquoise

Coast, was included in Mark Antony's wedding gift to Cleopatra, and included two of the seven ancient wonders of the world?

164.Which island in French Polynesia was the last port of call before the mutiny on the HMS Bounty, and also where the artist Paul Gauguin spent the last few years of his life?

165.Which island, roughly equidistant between North America and Asia, saw a key WWII battle in 1942, and is the only island in the Hawaiian archipelago that is not considered part of Hawaii?

166.The second largest of the Juan Fernández Islands off the coast of Chile was renamed to what in 1966, in a bid to reflect its literary heritage and draw tourism to the island?

167.Which volcanic archipelago, now a part of Ecuador, is known for its range of endemic species, and was studied by Charles Darwin?

168.Which one of the Solomon Islands saw heavy fighting in 1942-43, ending in an Allied victory?

169.Which TV series stars Kristen Bell as the lead character, a teen detective solving crimes in the fictional town of Neptune, California?

170.Which detective portrayed by Rajit Kapur in a 1993 TV series first appeared in the episode 'Satyanweshi', which is also a moniker he gives himself?

171.Which detective portrayed by Nathan Fillion stars as the titular character, a best-selling mystery novelist who solves unusual crimes in

New York City?

172.Which detective, the eponymous lead portrayed by Peter Falk, was known for his catchphrase 'Just one more thing'?

173.Which newspaper, whose name means 'truth', was the official newspaper of the Communist Party of the Soviet Union?

174.Which newspaper, the top-selling daily in India as per the 2019 Indian Readership Survey, was first published in Jhansi in 1942, suspended after the Quit India movement, and then relaunched from Kanpur in 1947?

175.Which British newspaper, published since 1855, uses the motto "Was, is, and will be", and counts Boris Johnson and Graham Norton among former columnists?

176.What term is used to describe a major national newspaper with large circulation, whose editorial and news-gathering functions are considered authoritative and independent? The USA's *Wall Street Journal*, India's *The Hindu*, and the UK's *The Guardian* all fall in this category.

177.Which manga features the brothers Edward and Alphonse Elric, who are searching for the philosopher's stone to restore their bodies after a failed attempt to bring their mother back to life?

178.Which manga features Monkey D. Luffy, a boy whose body gained the properties of rubber after unintentionally eating a Devil Fruit, and who is seeking the titular treasure?

179.Which manga is set in a post-apocalyptic and

futuristic "Neo-Tokyo", more than two decades after a mysterious explosion destroyed the city? Cyberpunk anime became popular thanks to its movie adaptation.

180.Which manga by Osamu Tezuka features a young android with human emotions, who is created by Umataro Tenma after the recent death of his son Tobio?

181.Which fictional island country, separated from the island of the story title by a 730m channel, parodies 18th century France, and was a place of refuge for Big-Endian exiles?

182.In which fictional country in Central Europe does Rudolf Rassendyll impersonate the kidnapped King Rudolf V?

183.Which fictional banana republic in South America has its capital at Los Dopicos, which is then renamed to Tapiocapolis and back again?

184.Which fictional East European country was the target of a US bombing campaign using Stark-manufactured bombs? Its capital Novi Grad was destroyed by Ultron using a vibranium machine.

185.Which cyclist, known as one of the inventors of the modern mountain bike, sold his eponymous bike company to Trek Bicycles in 2010?

186.Which bicycle manufacturer is named after the California county it is based out of, and names its bikes after locations in the country such as Presidio, Muirwoods and San Quentin?

187. Which Milan-based bike manufacturer that opened in 1885 shares its name with the last name of the actress who played the Bond girl in *From Russia with Love*?

188. Which India-based bike manufacturer shares its name with a browser and an endangered Himalayan mammal?

189. Which American bicycle brand that shares its name with a type of textile sponsors the five-time Ironman champion Daniela Ryf?

190. In the 1984 TV series about the 1932-33 Bodyline Test series between England and Australia, who portrayed the England captain Douglas Jardine?

191. Don Bradman missed one of the five tests in the Bodyline series but still managed to top the run charts for Australia. Wally Hammond and which other batter topped the charts for England?

192. Which cricketer scored a hundred on debut in the first test of the Bodyline series, but took no further part in the series due to his dissent against Bodyline tactics?

193. Which Australian wicketkeeper, who holds a record 52 stumpings in Test cricket, had his skull fractured by Harold Larwood in the third test of the Bodyline series?

194. What widely consumed beige / green seed, native to Central Asia, shows up in archaeological records as far back as 6750 BC, and is documented by Pliny the Elder as native to Syria?

195.What seed, native to West & North Africa, has a significant proportion of caffeine, & is used as a flavoring ingredient in carbonated soft drinks?

196.What seed, the state nut of Alabama, Arkansas, California, and Texas, is commonly used to make an eponymous pie, a traditional southern US dish?

197.What nut, that takes 5 to 24 months in the soil to mature, gets its name from the Gothic akran, which meant "fruit of the unenclosed land"?

198.Who, in a Charles Dickens novella, is visited by the ghost of his former business partner Jacob Marley, as well as the spirits of Christmas Past, Present and Yet to Come?

199.Where does Father Christmas meet the Pevensies and give them weapons, a place earlier denied access to him by the White Witch's magic? The setting is a 1950 novel by CS Lewis.

200.The Royal Ruby is hidden in what food item, in the eponymous Hercule Poirot story written by Agatha Christie?

201.Who tries to steal Christmas from the town of Whoville, in the children's story by Dr. Seuss?

202.Harry and Marv suffer much physical abuse when they attempt to rob the McCallister house in Chicago in which movie?

203.Kris Kringle plays a department store Santa Claus who claims to be the real Santa, for a Christmas miracle on which road, in the

Hollywood classic?

204. Which Robert Zemeckis directed motion-capture computer-animated film features children on a train going to meet Santa Claus at the North Pole?

205. Which Christmas themed movie stars Billy Bob Thornton as a con man dressing up and robbing malls over the country?

206. The duo of Lloyd Christmas and Harry Dunne feature in what movie series, where their actions always result in unexpected and often hilarious results?

207. Denise Richards plays Dr. Christmas Jones, an American nuclear physicist, in which James Bond film?

208. What disease, also called the 'Royal disease' due to its prevalence in many European royal families, is also called Christmas disease as it was first described in the patient Stephen Christmas?

209. Which former province of South Africa, later merged with the KwaZulu territory, got its name from the Portuguese word for Christmas, because Vasco da Gama saw its coast on Christmas Day in 1497?

210. Christmas Island, located 350km south of Java, was named by Captain William Mynors on Christmas Day in 1643. It has many endemic species due to its geographic isolation. Which country is it now a part of?

Set 5 Answers

1. Sampadi
2. Kushadhwaja
3. Mahiravana
4. Manthara
5. Stefan Edberg
6. Margaret Court
7. Steffi Graf
8. Martina Hingis
9. Spain
10. Horatio Nelson
11. Norway
12. George IV
13. Bowie Knife
14. Rampuri
15. Stiletto
16. Bayonet
17. Joseph Goebbels
18. William Henry Harrison
19. Charan Singh
20. Mexico
21. The First War of Independence
22. Isaac Asimov
23. Carbon
24. Gil-Galad
25. Albert Michelson
26. Harshavardhana
27. Al-Biruni
28. Vijayanagar
29. Aurangzeb
30. Halloween
31. *Kabhie Khushi Kabhie Gham*

32. *Zanjeer*
33. *Chachi 420 / Avvai Shanmughi*
34. Narakasura
35. Ayodhya
36. Lakshmi
37. Mahavira
38. Dune
39. Acme
40. LexCorp
41. Weyland-Yutani
42. InGen
43. Canada
44. The Gambia
45. Liberia
46. Cinque Terre
47. Kandahar
48. Ghazni
49. Jalalabad
50. Herat
51. Padma Bhushan
52. Illustrated Weekly of India
53. Train to Pakistan
54. Sikhs
55. Noddy
56. Malory Towers
57. The Five Find-Outers and Dog
58. Amelia Jane
59. Cholula
60. Damascus
61. Jericho
62. Varanasi
63. Luxor

64. Istanbul / Constantinople
65. Indraprastha
66. Leningrad
67. Port Elizabeth
68. Ruy Lopez
69. Anatoly Karpov
70. Jose Raul Capablanca
71. Mikail Botvinnik
72. Generation gap
73. Gini coefficient
74. Digital divide
75. Uncontacted and nomadic people
76. Poland
77. France
78. Bangladesh
79. UAE
80. Old Goa
81. Kadamba
82. National Institute of Oceanography
83. Bijapur
84. Charles Correa
85. *I Am Number Four*
86. *Catch-22*
87. *Nineteen Eighty-Four*
88. *The Two Towers*
89. Ujesh Ranchod
90. Mohammed Rafique
91. Cameron White
92. Hansie Cronje
93. Balaclava
94. Beret
95. Jinnah

96. Deerstalker
97. *Tron: Legacy*
98. *Highlander*
99. Pink Floyd
100. *Fight Club*
101. Chrysanthemum
102. Rose
103. Mayflower
104. Lily of the Valley
105. Tulip
106. CV Raman
107. JC Bose
108. Anil Kakodkar
109. CNR Rao
110. Keke Rosberg
111. Mika Hakkinen
112. Kimi Raikkonen
113. Valtteri Bottas
114. Czechoslovakia
115. Italy
116. Bulgaria
117. England
118. Angola
119. Cuba
120. Haiti
121. Israel
122. Kathryn Fitzpatrick
123. Taunton
124. Chakda Express
125. Chennai
126. New Zealand
127. Senegal

128. Cameroon
129. East Germany
130. USA
131. *The Man from U.N.C.L.E.*
132. Mammy Two Shoes
133. Zoot Suit
134. Franz Liszt
135. Yamuna
136. Lahore
137. Peacock Throne
138. Jama Masjid
139. *Piper at the Gates of Dawn*
140. *Animals*
141. *The Wall*
142. *The Division Bell*
143. Heart
144. Christian Barnard
145. Rejection
146. Transplant between identical twins who were genetically similar
147. Drone
148. The Corrs
149. Bihari Brothers
150. The Beach Boys
151. The Allman Brothers Band
152. *Streets of Philadelphia*
153. *New York Minute*
154. *Brighton Rock*
155. *Kashmir*
156. Mount Gay rum with soda
157. Macallan
158. Mint Julep

159. Black Velvet
160. Nice
161. Red Sea
162. Mexico
163. Turkey
164. Tahiti
165. Midway Island
166. Robinson Crusoe Island
167. Galapagos
168. Guadalcanal
169. Veronica Mars
170. Byomkesh Bakshi
171. Richard Castle
172. Columbo
173. Pravda
174. Dainik Jagran
175. The Daily Telegraph
176. Newspaper of record
177. Fullmetal Alchemist
178. One Piece
179. Akira
180. Astro Boy
181. Blefuscu
182. Ruritania
183. San Theodoros
184. Sokovia
185. Gary Fischer
186. Marin
187. Bianchi
188. Firefox
189. Felt
190. Hugo Weaving

191. Herbert Sutcliffe
192. Iftikhar Ali Khan Pataudi
193. Bert Oldfield
194. Pistachio
195. Kola nut
196. Pecan
197. Acorn
198. Ebenezer Scrooge
199. Narnia
200. Christmas Pudding
201. Grinch
202. *Home Alone*
203. 34th Street
204. *The Polar Express*
205. Bad Santa
206. *Dumb and Dumber*
207. *The World Is Not Enough*
208. Hemophilia
209. Natal
210. Australia

THEMED QUESTIONS

- Theme 1
    a. Which 2006 espionage novel by Frederick Forsyth features an attempt by western agencies to pass off a Westerner into a terrorist operation?

    b. In American football, what name is given to a player who receives the snapped ball directly from the line of scrimmage, and then kicks the football to the opposing team so as to limit any field position advantage?

    c. How do we commonly know the *Drosophila melanogaster*, which is found in all continents, and is a common pest in homes, restaurants, and other places where food is served?

    d. What species, often considered a pest in cities due to its feces, has been domesticated for hundreds of years, with some varieties also used to carry messages?

- Theme 2
  a. Which American writer is best known for his short stories 'Rip Van Winkle' and 'The Legend of Sleepy Hollow'?
  b. Which monarch reigned for almost 64 years, and is still associated with strict standards of personal morality?
  c. Which director & former actress won the Oscar for Best Original Screenplay for the 2003 movie *Lost in Translation*?
  d. Considered by many as 'famous only for being famous', which media personality, singer, & actress' first book *Confessions of an Heiress* was a New York Times best seller?

- Theme 3
  a. The line of monarchs of Great Britain from 1714 to 1901, starting with George I and ending with Victoria, belonged to which Royal House?
  b. Which actor, with roles in movies like *Wanted*, *Moneyball* and *Zero Dark Thirty*, played Star-Lord in the Marvel movies?
  c. Which mathematician and physicist, knighted for his work on the Transatlantic telegraph project in 1866, is best known for his work in thermodynamics, and has a unit of temperature named in his honor?
  d. Which novel by SJ Bennett features

Queen Elizabeth II as a detective investigating a death at a royal residence in the English county of Berkshire?

- Theme 4
  a. Which paint pigment, occurring naturally in the mineral crocoite, is commonly associated with American school buses, and sounds like a book by Aldous Huxley?
  b. Which endangered animal is found in coniferous & temperate forests in the Himalayas, feeds mainly on bamboo, and featured as Shifu in the *Kung Fu Panda* movies?
  c. Which word, meaning 'journey' in Swahili, entered the English language in the 1850s thanks to Richard Francis Burton, and is now used to refer to a journey to observe wild animals?
  d. What is the common name of Enhanced GPRS, or Enhanced Data for Global Evolution?

- Theme 5
  a. Which character, known for his trademark zigzag patterned shirt, first appeared in print in 1950? The command module of the Apollo 10 space mission was also named after him.
  b. In *Harry Potter and the Order of the Phoenix*, what number do Mr. Weasley and Harry dial to enter the Ministry of Magic in

London via the visitor's entrance in an abandoned red telephone box? Why this specific number?

c. *The Hitchhiker's Guide to the Galaxy* is a fictional guidebook in the book series of the same name by Douglas Adams. What words are printed on its cover?

d. Sir Isaac Newton computed it to be 298 meters per second, about 15% too low. William Derham measured it in 1709 as 342.8 meters per second, very close to the current accepted benchmark (which of course varies by temperature and pressure). What were they attempting to measure?

- Theme 6
  a. The Mayan city of Tikal, declared a UNESCO World Heritage site in 1979, is located in which present-day country?
  b. Which country became landlocked after the War of the Pacific, fought from 1879 to 1884, in which its neighbor took over its nitrate-rich coastal regions?
  c. Which country, the only state in history to win independence through a slave revolt, was under French rule from 1697 to 1804?
  d. Which African country, whose only official language is Portuguese, derived its name from Mussa Bin Bique, an Arab

trader who visited and lived there?

- Theme 7
  a. Whose assassination in 1914 by Gavrilo Princip is considered the most immediate cause of World War I?
  b. Which America artist and director is best known for his paintings of *Campbell's Soup Cans* and his association with the rock band *The Velvet Underground*?
  c. What device uses a moving belt to accumulate electric charge on a hollow metal globe on top of an insulated column, thus creating very high electric potentials?
  d. Which English agriculturist from Berkshire invented a horse-drawn seed drill in 1700, and is considered as one of the drivers of the British Agricultural Revolution of the 18th century?

- Theme 8
  a. Known for his trademark 'Rubber legs' dancing style, which singer made his film debut in 1956, served in the military, and in 1973, gave the first concert by a solo artist to be broadcast around the world?
  b. Since 2005, which song has been played just before midnight at the Times Square ball drop on New Year's Eve in New York City?
  c. Which scandal, named after the complex

where the events occurred, eventually led to the resignation of US President Richard Nixon in 1974?

d. Which restaurant chain first opened in 1996 in Monterey, California, and is named after a duo from a hugely popular 1994 film?

- Theme 9

    a. What work of art was completed between 1508 and 1512, and includes nine scenes from the Book of Genesis, including the *Creation of Adam*?

    b. Which painting, a half-length portrait painted in oil, is widely believed to be of the noblewoman Lisa Gherardini, the wife of Francesco del Giocondo?

    c. Which work of art, painted between 1509 and 1511 in the Vatican, is known for its accurate perspective projection, and includes Plato and Aristotle, among others, as its subjects?

    d. Which Renaissance sculptor is best known for his statue of *St. John the Baptist* in Siena, Italy?

- Theme 10

    a. What was the name of the mountain peak Denali, the tallest in North America, from 1917 to 2015?

    b. Which motor brand, started in 1917 by Henry Leland, was acquired by Ford in

1922 as its luxury vehicle division?

c. Which character was first created in 1976, and is known for its laziness, disdain of Mondays, and love for coffee and lasagna?

d. Which Oscar winning Oliver Stone film starred Kevin Bacon, Kevin Costner, Gary Oldman, & Tommy Lee Jones?

- Theme 11

    a. Which film, also Meryl Streep's debut, won Vanessa Redgrave a 1977 Best Supporting Actress Oscar and Jane Fonda a Best Actress Oscar?

    b. Which 2016 animated film, titled *Leap!* in the USA, focuses on an orphan girl in 1880s France, trying to get into a production of *The Nutcracker*?

    c. In Rudyard Kipling's *The Jungle Book*, what kind of animal is Kaa?

    d. Which a population of 147.7 million, which is the world's most populous island?

- Theme 12

    a. What one-word term was used to describe the German bombing campaign against Britain in 1940 and 1941?

    b. How do we know the ancient city of Swenett, later called Syne, a south-facing frontier town of the ancient kingdom? It was known for its stone quarries which supplied stone to famous monuments to the north but is now known for modern stonework instead.

c. The fifth Caliph of the Abbasid Dynasty, Haroun al-Rashid, features in several stories in *One Thousand and One Nights*. Which modern-day country was his Caliphate based out of, as described in the *Sindbad the Sailor* stories?

d. What luxury overnight express train ran from Calais to the French Riviera from 1886 to 2003, until it was replaced by the much faster TGV?

- Theme 13
    a. What one word connects a European city, a character in Homer's *Iliad*, and a socialite heiress?

    b. The Bagan Empire grew out of a 9th century settlement until it was consolidated into a kingdom in 1044, lasting until a Mongol invasion in 1287. What is the former name of the present-day country in which this Empire existed?

    c. What town, midway between Manchester and Liverpool, was incorporated in 1246 through a Royal charter, and is a key point on the Leeds and Liverpool Canal?

    d. Which autonomous territory, formerly annexed by the first French Empire in 1812, unilaterally declared independence in 2017, leading to the country's Senate enforcing direct rule?

- Theme 14
    a. What game, first documented in the 1700s, is also known popularly as *Patience* or *Klondike*, and is played by a single player?
    b. Which company, founded in 1909, entered India in 1981 as a minor partner in partnership with the Government of India, later becoming major shareholder in 2003?
    c. What tournament, now held every two years, was first held in 1927 at the Worcester Country Club and involved participants from Great Britain and Ireland? It is notable for the absence of prize money to any participant; despite the high prestige and coverage the event receives.
    d. What name connects a psychological complex, a Greek mythological character after whom the complex is named, and a Marvel Comics character played by Jennifer Garner?

- Theme 15
    a. Which writer, best known for his children's stories which typically involve adult villains bullying the protagonists, also wrote the screenplay for the James

Bond film *You Only Live Twice*?

b. Which actor, best known for a role where he taught the 'Force', won the Best Actor Academy Award for a movie set on the Burma Railway?

c. Which American actor and entrepreneur won his only Academy Award for Best Actor for his role in the 1986 movie *The Color of Money*?

d. Which actor, often referred to as the 'King of Hollywood', is known for his roles in the movies *It Happened One Night*, *Mutiny on the Bounty*, and *Gone with the Wind*?

- Theme 16

  a. What two-word term connects an extra-terrestrial vampire in the DC Comics universe, a former English monarch's nickname, and a vodka-based cocktail?

  b. Which Biblical character was portrayed by Harvey Keitel in the 1988 Martin Scorsese film *The Last Temptation of Christ*?

  c. What word connects a character in the GI Joe universe, a two-handed Scottish broadsword, and an anti-personnel mine?

  d. What term is used to describe a chemical product used industrially or domestically to remove color from a fabric or fiber, or to clean or to remove stains? Chlorine and peroxides are commonly used in these products.

- Theme 17
    a. Who, heralded as the patron saint of the Third Republic, is most commonly depicted on horseback, tearing his cloak into two to clothe a beggar in winter?
    b. By what name is the Virgin Mary referred to in Mexico, after a series of visions seen in a Mexico City suburb by Juan Diego in 1531?
    c. What one word connects the name of a Black Sabbath album, a science fiction novel by Alan Dean Foster, and a gathering of individuals meeting after a long time?
    d. Which archipelago in the South Pacific Ocean includes the Grande Terre, the Loyalty Islands, the Chesterfield Islands, the Isle of Pines, and the Belep Islands?

- Theme 18
    a. What soft drink was first introduced as 'Brad's Drink' in North Carolina in 1893, and renamed in 1898 in line with new advertising claiming it aided digestion?
    b. Which Indian conglomerate, now comprising over 100 enterprises, took off as a trading firm in 1868, expanding into cotton mills, hotels, & steel?
    c. Which Indian fantasy sports platform, founded by Harsh Jain and Bhavit Shet in 2008, was the first Indian gaming

company to become a unicorn in 2019?

d. Which technology company is the official smartphone brand of the 2018 and 2022 FIFA World Cups, & uses its proprietary Origin OS operating system in its India products?

- Theme 19
    a. Whose 63-year long reign saw events such as the Great Irish Famine, the First War of Indian Independence, and the first Olympics Games?
    b. What name connects a supermarket chain in the Czech Republic, a short story by Leo Tolstoy, a town in New South Wales, and a famous physicist?
    c. Which king of England abdicated the throne in 1936 to marry the American divorcee, Wallis Simpson?
    d. Which sovereign state got its independence from the United Kingdom in 1961, becoming a republic within the Commonwealth a year later? It ceased to exist in 1964, when it merged with the offshore archipelago nation off its coast, to form a new unified country (with a new name).

- Theme 20
    a. Which actor, known for movies like Dabangg and Simmba, won the Special Humanitarian Action Award from the

UN for his humanitarian work during the Covid-19 pandemic?

b. Which actor made his Bollywood debut in the 1996 movie Barsaat along with Twinkle Khanna?

c. What was the screen name of Bollywood actor Harikishan Giri Goswami, who was known for directing and acting in movies with patriotic themes?

d. Which Indian actor started his career with the Bollywood movie *Phool Aur Kaante*?

- Theme 21

a. Which country, locally called Cymru, gets its name from the Brythonic word 'combrogi', which translates to "fellow-countrymen"? The more common name of the country derives from a Proto-Germanic word meaning "Roman".

b. Though Hyundai purportedly named this car brand after a Greek island which is also the site of an ancient civilization, the same word in Latin means *chalk*. What brand?

c. What historic region, now part of Russia, enjoyed independence due to its being midway between the Moscow, Novgorod and Kazan powers? The name also refers to a hair treatment which sets hair into waves.

d. Which English County, the only one to border Cornwall, is the setting for the Arthur Conan Doyle novel *The Hound of the Baskervilles?*

- Theme 22
    a. Which highly territorial apex predator is found across large parts of Asia? Its Caspian, Javan and Bali sub-species are now extinct.
    b. What one word connects a defective product, the last name of Tina Fey's character on *30 Rock*, and a popular fruit with a sour taste?
    c. What word comes from the Latin for 'one who nourishes', and is known for proponents such as Florence Nightingale?
    d. Which group of mammals within the order Cetacea has two subcategories – baleen and toothed?

- Theme 23
    a. Which Greek goddess of agriculture and vegetation was abducted by Hades, with her abduction believed to be the reason for winter, and her temporary return to the surface the reason for spring?
    b. The kings of which French dynasty were distinguished by their long hair, decreeing that one with hair cut short could not be king, and ruled from the 5th century until 751, when Pepin the Short, the father of Charlemagne, deposed their last king?
    c. Which company was co-founded in 1977 as Software Development Laboratories?

It changed its name to Relational Software, Inc in 1979, and its current name in 1983.

d. Which Greek god is associated with sleep and dreams, and appears in dreams in human form? It is also the name of a Neil Gaiman protagonist.

- Theme 24
    a. Which city, on the banks of the Shipra River, was the capital of the Avanti Kingdom, and is also mentioned as the capital of the Western province of the Mauryan Empire in Asokan edicts?
    b. Which city is known for Annie Besant founding the Central Hindu College in 1898, and for the Hindu belief that dying in and being cremated in this city allows one to escape the cycle of rebirth?
    c. Which city was founded by the King of Amer in 1727, to accommodate the rising population and water scarcity in Amer?
    d. The foundation stone of which city was laid by George V of England during the 1911 Delhi Durbar, with the city being designed by Edwin Lutyens and Herbert Baker?

- Theme 25:
    a. Which musician, better known for his work as part of a band, released the single 'My Sweet Lord' in 1970?

b. Who played the titular Mrs. Robinson in the 1967 movie *The Graduate* & the Simon & Garfunkel song of the same name?

c. Who was portrayed on-screen in an Academy Award nominated role by Christian Bale, in the movie Vice?

d. Which Australian-born activist lived in the Ecuador Embassy in London from 2012 to 2019, while fighting legal battles with multiple governments?

- Theme 26:
    a. What name is given to the Japanese art of appreciating incense, and using incense within a codified structure?

    b. What word connects a colloquial term for the bridge connecting an airport to an airplane, a brand of chocolate by Cadbury, and a vulgar hand gesture?

    c. Which Pulitzer and Nobel Prize winning author spent most of her childhood and early adulthood in Zhenjiang and Nanjing before returning to the USA at the age of 43?

    d. What term is used to describe grasses that disperse their seeds as a unit, because they resemble the hind appendage of an animal of the dog family?

- Theme 27:
    a. Which water body, which includes the Bay of Bothnia and the Gulf of Riga,

among others, stretches from 53°N to 66°N latitude, and from 10°E to 30°E longitude?

b. Which former country was first formed in 1918, after the merger of multiple portions of the former Ottoman and Austro-Hungarian Empires, with Peter I as its first sovereign? It got its more commonly used name in 1929.

c. What nickname did the artist and sculptor Domenikos Theotokopoulos, a key Renaissance figure who worked in Rome and Toledo, adopt?

d. Which Mario Puzo novel, published in 1984, is based on the life of the bandit Salvatore Giuliano, and set on a Mediterranean island?

- Theme 28:

  a. Which Oscar nominated film starring Nicole Kidman shares its name with a cat species depicted in a Disney recreation of the Hamlet story?

  b. Which animal of the species *Accipitridae* is found across all continents, with types such as harpy, golden, crested, martial, pygmy, steppe, and bald?

  c. Which animal, also a character in the classic book *The Wind in the Willows*, belongs to the family which also includes otters, weasels, and wolverines?

  d. Which Netflix TV series, featuring Tahar

Rahim as Charles Sobhraj, shares its name with a Biblical creature considered responsible for the fall of man?

- Theme 29:
  a. The earliest evidence of this food item is from China 4,000 years ago. Which item, a staple food in many countries especially in SE Asia and known best for its instant variant?
  b. Which British household appliance brand was started by two former British Army and Morphy Richards engineers, and is known primarily for its kettles and coffee pots, though it makes and sells all kitchen appliances?
  c. Traditional animation, in which each frame is drawn by hand, is known by which other name, indicative of the number of dimensions in the art?
  d. Which fictional musician is based on Keith Richards, plays the bass, and made a deal with the devil to become a famous musician, adopting the middle name Faust in the process?

- Theme 30:
  a. What material was invented in 1912 and got its name because it was marketed as a substitute for a silicate mineral used as an insulator?
  b. Which Swiss entrepreneur who inherited

his father's hammer mill in 1869, invented instant soup in 1886? The company merged with Nestle in 1947.

c. Who served as US President during the Great Depression, until his defeat to Franklin Roosevelt in the 1932 election?

d. Which corporation, known for its print and digital document products, also famously invented the desktop GUI and mouse which were then adopted and popularized by Apple?

- Theme 31:
  a. Which cricketer, signed on as an overseas player by Warwickshire in 1994, was the last person to score a quadruple century in cricket, before Sam Northeast achieved the feat in 2022?

  b. Which British Prime Minister, the only one to have been assassinated, and also the only attorney-general to become PM, shared his last name with a legendary knight?

  c. Which Anglo-Saxon name, literally meaning a wealthy member of the canine family, is also the name of the Gym Leader at Snowbelle City's Gym in the Pokemon universe?

  d. What common currency, used in the Late Middle Ages in the Holy Roman Empire, had a higher silver content and was thus lighter in color, giving it its name, which means 'white' in Latin?

- Theme 32:
  a. Which freedom activist, imprisoned during the Quit India movement, was Minister of Information and Broadcasting during the Emergency, and also served as Ambassador to the Soviet Union before taking on a bigger political role in 1997?
  b. Who, imprisoned during the Emergency, served as Member of Parliament from 1962 to 2007 (except from 1984-89), & is remembered for his minority government failing to pass the Budget in 1991?
  c. After which former politician is the Lucknow International Airport, formerly called the Amausi airport, named?
  d. Which politician, also the 41st Raja Bahadur of Manda in Uttar Pradesh, saw his government fall after his opposition to the 1990 Ram Rath Yatra?

- Theme 33:
  a. What connects an English football club, a West Side neighborhood in New York, and a former first daughter of the USA?
  b. Known as the 'Blue City' and featuring in the movie *The Dark Knight Rises*, which city is centered around the Mehrangarh Fort?
  c. The game of polo runs for 1.5-2 hours

and is divided into 4 to 8 seven-minute sessions. What is each of these sessions called, a word which sounds like a spot of dizziness in Hindi?

d. Which castle in Aberdeenshire, Scotland, has been one of the British family's residences since 1852, and is owned privately by the Crown?

- Theme 34:

a. Which doctor, after whom the *Institute and Hospital for Tropical Diseases* in the UK is named, helped discover the working of a disease which claimed 600,000+ deaths in 2020?

b. Who, born in Bombay, was named after a reservoir in Staffordshire where his parents met? He is best remembered for a collection of stories, set in Seonee among other places.

c. How do we better know Tenzin Gyatso, who fled to Indian in 1959, and who is believed to be an incarnation of *Avalokiteswara*, the *Bodhisattva of Compassion*?

d. Who, in 1928 at the age of 18, joined the Sisters of Loreto in Ireland to learn English and become a missionary? A year later, she moved to the country where she would spend the rest of her life.

- Theme 35:

a. Which Kiwi tennis player, who died aged 31 in World War I, won 11 Grand Slam titles, and also won the Davis Cup four times representing Australasia?

b. All we know about him is that his last name was Briggs and his first name started with H. He lived in Paris and hence qualified, even though he was British by citizenship. He was also a member of a French Club, which helped (it was a requirement until 1925). What is his only claim to fame?

c. After whom is the men's singles trophy at the Australian Open tennis championship named?

d. Which six-time Grand Slam champion won the Men's Singles as well as Doubles events in tennis at the 1900 Summer Olympics? He teamed up with his brother Reginald, himself a four-time Wimbledon champion, in the doubles.

- Theme 36:
  a. Which country, comprising 32 atolls and one coral island, is the only country to be located in all four cardinal hemispheres?

  b. Which country existed as an unrecognized republic from 1965 to 1979, after the predominantly white government issued a Unilateral Declaration of Independence from the United Kingdom to delay the transition to black majority rule?

c. Which self-governing island country in the South Pacific comprises of 15 islands with the capital at Avarua, and exists in free association with New Zealand?

d. Which Atlantic archipelago, 480km from the nearest continental land mass, has its capital at Stanley, and was named by English captain John Strong in 1690, after the sponsor of his expedition?

- Theme 37:
  a. Which Bollywood film by David Dhawan features Priyanka Chopra, Salman Khan, & Akshay Kumar, & features a marriage proposal in an India-Pak cricket game?

  b. Which 2014 film featured Adam Sandler and Drew Barrymore as single parents forced to stay together at an African safari resort with their children?

  c. In which film, based on the 1985 English movie Brewster's Millions, does the protagonist played by Naseeruddin Shah have to spend 30 crore rupees in 30 days, in order to win a a 300-crore inheritance?

  d. Which Bollywood film had Akshay Kumar play a fast bowler who wants to play for England, while his father (played by Rishi Kapoor) keeps him away from cricket?

- Theme 38:
  a. Who does Oberon call upon to concoct a

magical juice using the flower called 'love-in-idleness', which when applied to the eyelids of a sleeping person, will make them fall in love with the first living person they perceive on waking?

b. *The Winds of Winter* is the long awaited (but as of 2021, unreleased) installment in the *Song of Ice and Fire series* by which author?

c. Which film, also Ingrid Bergman's final film role, heavily features Chopin's *Prelude No. 2 in A minor*?

d. Norwegian author Karl Ove Knausgard became known worldwide for six autobiographical novels titled *My Struggle*. In 2015-2016, what series of four books did he publish, also autobiographical in nature?

- Theme 39:

  a. Which landscape painter, known for works such as *The Fighting Temeraire*, famously rowed a boat into the Thames in 1841, so he could not be counted as present at any property in that year's census?

  b. Which famous author's posthumously published works include *Northanger Abbey*, *Persuasion*, and *Lady Susan*?

  c. After whom is a 2017 law in the United Kingdom, that retroactively pardoned men cautioned or convicted under historical legislation that outlawed homosexual acts, informally named?

d. Which English statesman and leader was awarded the Nobel Prize in Literature in 1953, for his "mastery of historical and biographical description" and oratorial output?

- Theme 40:
    a. Which fictional monkey, the title character of a series of popular children's books written by Margret and H. A. Rey, is described as "a good little monkey, and always very curious"?
    b. Which monthly women's entertainment & fashion magazine was first seen in 1886 as a family magazine, before switching to its current avatar in 1965?
    c. What name connects an anthropomorphic mouse with the part-name of an ice-cream company bought by Unilever in 2000?
    d. Which sprinter broke the women's 100m sprint Olympic record at the 2020 Games?

- Theme 41:
    a. Which war film set mainly in a German prisoner-of-war camp includes, among other things, a motorcycle chase sequence featuring Steve McQueen?
    b. Which 1972 film starring Laurence Olivier and Michael Caine was remade in

2007, with Caine playing the role played by Olivier in the original?

c. Which historical drama that won seven Academy awards was based on a British army officer serving in the Middle East during World War I?

d. Which 1957 courtroom drama starring Henry Fonda was remade in Hindi in 1987 with the title *Ek Ruka Hua Faisla*?

- Theme 42:

    a. Which 1955 movie, literally meaning 'Song of the Little Road', was partly funded by the local government, who misunderstood the nature of the film, recording the grant as being for "roads improvement"?

    b. The term refers to any vehicle which uses two or more sources of power and was first seen in the 1901 Lohner-Porsche. The term became popular with the 1997 launch of the Toyota Prius. What's the good word?

    c. Which time zone contains the Canadian regions of Alberta & Yukon, & the US states of Colorado, Montana, Utah, New Mexico, Wyoming, & Arizona? Other states partly exist in this time zone as well.

    d. What began during the early 1970s in southern California, when children began racing their bicycles on dirt tracks, inspired by motocross riders of the time?

- Theme 43:
    a. Which city in Gujarat state of India was formerly part of the princely state of Nawanagar, and is known for the world's largest petrochemical complex run by Reliance Industries?
    b. Which city in southern Rajasthan state of India, also known for receiving the most rain in Rajasthan, gets its name from the abundance of bamboo forests in the area?
    c. Which town, a sub-division of Gurugram district in India, was the headquarters of a former princely state? The main palace is now owned by a popular Bollywood actor.
    d. Which city in Andhra Pradesh in India was formerly a part of the Kalinga kingdom, & was later ruled by the Pasupati dynasty?

- Theme 44:
    a. What word, meaning an overwhelming force, derives from a form of Vishnu worshipped on the Eastern coast of India?
    b. Which chess opening that starts with the moves '1. d4 d5 2. c4' is also the name of a Netflix miniseries starring Anya Taylor-Joy?
    c. Which American TV series, that ran from 2013-16, is based in a small town of the

same name, and features an ex-con who assumes the identity of Lucas Hood, the town's murdered sheriff?

d. What statue of the Greek sun-god Helios was built in 280 BC by Chares of Lindos, and was considered one of the Seven Wonders of the Ancient World?

- Theme 45:
    a. What crustacean has varieties such as snow, blue, mud, robber, and spider?

    b. What animal species has variants such as harpy, crowned, golden and bald, among others?

    c. The gemstone chrysoberyl, an aluminate of beryllium, has a variant whose opalescence reminds one of a body part of an animal. What is its common name?

    d. What object is left in the bed of movie producer Jack Woltz in the movie *The Godfather*, to show him that the Corleones mean business?

- Theme 46:
    a. Which country, known for a desert with the same name, sees the least rainfall among all sub-Saharan countries?

    b. Which present-day African country, with its capital at Lome, was a trading center for slaves, and was controlled by France from the end of WWI to 1960?

    c. Which African country's flag has a

diagonal black line representing the Swahili people, bordered by yellow lines indicating its mineral wealth? The portion of the flag above the diagonal lines is green, for the natural vegetation, and below the diagonal lines is blue, for the Indian Ocean.

d. Which colony, that lasted from 1884 to 1916, included northern parts of Gabon and the Congo with western parts of the Central African Republic, southwestern parts of Chad and far eastern parts of Nigeria? It shares a phonetic similarity with another present-day nation, which it also comprised.

- Theme 47:
    a. Which structure, the oldest such in India, was commissioned by Emperor Ashoka at the place his wife hailed from?
    b. Which 13th century stone temple attributed to the Eastern Ganga dynasty, is shaped as a chariot with wheels and horses?
    c. What structure was commissioned by Shah Jahan in 1638, when he decided to shift his capital from Agra to Delhi?
    d. Which stepwell, one of the largest of its kind, was built by the Chalukya King Bhima I, and is designed as an inverted temple showing the sanctity of water?

- Theme 48:
  a. Which 1977 song by the Bee Gees is about survival in the streets of New York?
  b. Which Guns N' Roses song, from their debut album *Appetite for Destruction*, talks about a place 'where the grass is green and the girls are pretty'?
  c. What name is given to a lubricant that is technically a soap emulsified with mineral or vegetable oil, with higher viscosity than oil, and thus used for mechanisms that need lubrication only infrequently?
  d. What term deriving from the cheap paper on which they were printed, was given to inexpensive magazines in the early 20th century? The term is also used to describe low quality literature.

- Theme 49:
  a. Who, along with his younger brother, lives in Bayport, NY and solves mysteries as an amateur detective?
  b. What baked item, commonly seen dunked in tea, was created by the London bakery Peek Freans in 1874 to commemorate the marriage of the Grand Duchess of Russia to the then Duke of Edinburgh?
  c. Who played Kitty Forman on the sitcom *That '70s Show*, and Alice Knight-Buffay on the third through fifth seasons of *Friends*?

d. Which fabric and fashion retailer with a 'Made to Measure' line began as a woolen mill in Thane, India in 1925?

- Theme 50:
    a. What is a match or season, in which typically all the ticket proceeds are given to a retiring player, to boost their income?
    b. What term was first used in the British newspaper *The Stage* in 1911, describing a woman named Nellie Perrier delivering ' _____ __ comic ditties in a charming & chic manner'? The blank is the answer.
    c. What was the name given to the scuba equipment invented in 1942-43 by Gagnan and Cousteau?
    d. What phrase, used to mock one's intellect, suggests that new thoughts can't enter one's head because of its similarity to a building material?

Theme Answers

- Theme 1: Nicknames of Aussie cricketers
    a. Afghan (Mark Waugh because he was the forgotten 'Waugh')
    b. Punter (Ricky Ponting)
    c. Fruit fly (Merv Hughes – considered the biggest pest in Australia)
    d. Pigeon (Glenn McGrath)

- Theme 2: Capital cities of countries
    a. Washington Irving = Washington DC, USA
    b. Queen Victoria = Victoria, Seychelles
    c. Sofia Coppola = Sofia, Bulgaria
    d. Paris Hilton = Paris, France

- Theme 3: Tie knots
    a. House of (Hanover)
    b. Chris (Pratt)
    c. Lord (Kelvin)
    d. The (Windsor) Knot

- Theme 4: Internet browsers
    a. Chrome (Yellow)
    b. Firefox (Red Panda)
    c. Safari
    d. Edge

- Theme 5: Singles by the band Coldplay
    a. Charlie Brown (from Peanuts)
    b. Magic (one has to dial 62442 to enter

the Ministry of Magic)
  c. Don't Panic
  d. Speed of Sound

- Theme 6: Countries with firearms on their national flags
  a. Guatemala
  b. Bolivia
  c. Haiti
  d. Mozambique

- Theme 7: Rock bands named after people
  a. Franz Ferdinand
  b. Andy Warhol (The Dandy Warhols)
  c. Van de Graff Generator
  d. Jethro Tull

- Theme 8: Events / things influenced by Forrest Gump in the eponymous movie
  a. Elvis Presley's dancing style
  b. *Imagine* by John Lennon
  c. Watergate Scandal
  d. Bubba Gump Shrimp Company

- Theme 9: Teenage Mutant Ninja Turtles
  a. Michelangelo painted the *Sistine Chapel*
  b. Da Vinci painted the *Mona Lisa*
  c. Raphael painted the *School of Athens*
  d. *St. John the Baptist* was sculpted by Donatello

- Theme 10: Assassinated US Presidents

a. The highest US peak is McKinley
b. The luxury car brand is Lincoln
c. The lazy cat is Garfield
d. The Oliver Stone movie is JFK

- Theme 11: Programming languages
  a. Julia
  b. Ballerina
  c. Python
  d. Java

- Theme 12: Settings for the openings of Hercule Poirot novels by Agatha Christie
  a. London Blitz (Taken at the Flood)
  b. Aswan (Death on the Nile)
  c. Iraq (Murder in Mesopotamia)
  d. Blue Train (Mystery of the Blue Train)

- Theme 13: Paris, Burma, Wigan, Catalonia. The connect is books by George Orwell.
  a. Down and Out in Paris and London
  b. Burmese Days
  c. The Road to Wigan Pier
  d. Homage to Catalonia

- Theme 14: Bond girls in James Bond films
  a. Solitaire (Live and Let Die)
  b. Suzuki (You Only Live Twice)
  c. Ryder (Dr. No)
  d. Elektra (The World is not Enough)

- Theme 15: Artists who played an active

military role in World War II
a.   Roald Dahl
b.   Alec Guinness
c.   Paul Newman
d.   Clark Gable

- Theme 16: Japanese manga
  a.   Bloody Mary
  b.   Judas
  c.   Claymore
  d.   Bleach

- Theme 17: French overseas territories
  a.   Saint Martin
  b.   Guadalupe
  c.   Reunion
  d.   New Caledonia

- Theme 18: IPL tournament sponsors
  a.   Pepsi
  b.   Tata
  c.   Dream11
  d.   Vivo

- Theme 19: Great Lakes in Africa
  a.   Victoria
  b.   Albert
  c.   Edward
  d.   Tanganyika

- Theme 20: Played Bhagat Singh on screen
  a.   Sonu Sood

    b.   Bobby Deol
    c.   Manoj Kumar
    d.   Ajay Devgn

- Theme 21: Geological time periods
  a. Cambrian (from Wales / Cambria)
  b. Cretaceous (from Creta / chalk)
  c. Permian (from the Perm regions)
  d. Devonian (from Devon)

- Theme 22: Types of sharks
  a. Tiger
  b. Lemon
  c. Nurse
  d. Whale

- Theme 23: Characters from the Matrix movie series
  a. Persephone
  b. Merovingian
  c. Oracle
  d. Morpheus

- Theme 24: Jantar Mantar sites
  a. Ujjain
  b. Varanasi
  c. Jaipur
  d. New Delhi

- Theme 25: *The Famous Five* by Enid Blyton
  a. 'George' Harrison
  b. 'Anne' Bancroft

    c.   'Dick' Cheney

    d.   'Julian' Assange

- Theme 26: Types of millet grains
  a. Kodo
  b. Finger
  c. Pearl
  d. Foxtail

- Theme 27: Opening defenses in chess
  a. Baltic
  b. Yugoslav
  c. Greco
  d. Sicilian

- Theme 28: House mascots at Hogwarts
  a. Lion
  b. Eagle
  c. Badger
  d. Serpent

- Theme 29: Band members of Gorillaz
  a. Noodle
  b. Russell Hobbs
  c. 2D
  d. Murdoc Niccals

- Theme 30: Genericized trademarks
  a. Formica
  b. Maggi
  c. Hoover
  d. Xerox

- Theme 31: The names of Dumbledore
  a. Brian (Lara)
  b. (Spencer) Percival
  c. Wulfric
  d. Albus

- Theme 32: Indian Prime Ministers with less than a year of total tenure
  a. IK Gujral
  b. Chandra Shekhar
  c. Charan Singh
  d. VP Singh

- Theme 33: Types of boots
  a. Chelsea
  b. Jodhpur
  c. Chukka
  d. Balmoral

- Theme 34: Non-Indian Nobel Laureates who did their life's work in India
  a. Ronald Ross
  b. Rudyard Kipling
  c. Dalai Lama
  d. Mother Teresa

- Theme 35: First winners of each Grand Slam to not be from the host country
  a. Anthony Wilding
  b. H. Briggs
  c. Norman Brookes

    d. Laurence Doherty

- Theme 36: Countries named after Britishers
    a. Kiribati (Gilbert Islands)
    b. Rhodesia
    c. Cook Islands
    d. Falkland Islands

- Theme 37: Cricketers who played themselves in movies
    a. Kapil Dev (Mujhse Shaadi Karogi)
    b. Dale Steyn (Blended)
    c. Sunil Gavaskar (Maalamaal)
    d. Andrew Symonds (Patiala House)

- Theme 38: Four seasons
    a. Robin 'Puck' Goodfellow (Midsummer Night's Dream)
    b. GRRM (The Winds of Winter)
    c. Autumn Sonata
    d. Karl Ove Knausgaard (Seasons)

- Theme 39: People on UK bank notes
    a. JMW Turner
    b. Jane Austen
    c. Alan Turing
    d. Winston Churchill

- Theme 40: Main characters in *Seinfeld*
    a. Curious 'George'
    b. 'Cosmo'politan
    c. Ben & 'Jerry'

  d.   'Elaine' Thompson-Herah

- Theme 41: Movies without women
  a.   The Great Escape
  b.   Sleuth
  c.   Lawrence of Arabia
  d.   12 Angry Men

- Theme 42: Types of bicycles
  a.   Road (Pather Panchali)
  b.   Hybrid
  c.   Mountain
  d.   BMX

- Theme 43: Royals who played cricket for India
  a.   Nawanagar
  b.   Bhanswara
  c.   Pataudi
  d.   Vizianagaram

- Theme 44: X-Men
  a.   Juggernaut
  b.   Queen's 'Gambit'
  c.   Banshee
  d.   Colossus (of Rhodes)

- Theme 45: Nebulae
  a.   Crab
  b.   Eagle
  c.   Cat's Eye
  d.   Horsehead

- Theme 46: Former German colonies
  a. Namibia
  b. Togo
  c. Tanzania
  d. Kamerun (Cameroon)

- Theme 47: Monuments on Indian Rupee currency notes
  a. Sanchi Stupa
  b. Sun Temple
  c. Red Fort
  d. Rani ki Vav

- Theme 48: John Travolta films
  a. Staying Alive
  b. Paradise City
  c. Grease
  d. Pulp Fiction

- Theme 49: Characters from *Everybody Loves Raymond*
  a. Frank (Hardy)
  b. Marie (biscuits)
  c. Debra (Jo Rupp)
  d. Raymond (Suitings)

- Theme 50: Jethro Tull albums
  a. *Benefit*
  b. *Stand Up*
  c. *Aqualung*
  d. *Thick as a Brick*

ABOUT THE AUTHOR

Sanat Pai Raikar is a husband and father, a triathlete, an avid quizzer, and a professional quizmaster, not necessarily in that order. He has written the definitive article on 'quiz' for the Encyclopaedia Britannica.

Sanat's quizzing journey began with school quizzes where he was very active in the inter-school quiz contests in Goa where he grew up. Sanat led the NIT Trichy quiz team to the quarterfinals of BBC World's University Challenge India.

Sanat co-founded Quizarre with his wife and partner-in-quiz Nirupama. Quizarre provides quiz, crossword and puzzle content to corporates, schools, entrance exam content aggregators and publications. Sanat hosts the annual Quiz Bowl of Goa, Goa's biggest school quiz.

His first quiz book, Three's A Quiz, was written from memory and published in 2021. This is his second quiz book.

Printed in Great Britain
by Amazon

18503867R00129